KITTY BAXTER was born in 1930 in Camberwell, South London, the third of five children, and was evacuated three times during the Second World War. After the war, Kitty went on to live a happy life in London and worked in Mayfair for over 35 years. She is very well known locally in Westminster, and regularly volunteers at the Imperial War Museum in Lambeth to share her story.

I'll Take That One

An Evacuee's Childhood

By Kitty Baxter

I'LL TAKE THAT ONE
AN EVACUEE'S CHILDHOOD

I'll Take That One

An Evacuee's Childhood

Kitty Baxter

Allison & Busby Limited
11 Wardour Mews
London W1F 8AN
allisonandbusby.com

First published in Great Britain by Allison & Busby in 2022

A CIP catalogue record for this book is available from
the British Library.

First Edition
ISBN 978-0-7490-2839-8

Typeset in 11.5/19.5pt Sabon LT Std
by Typo•glyphix, Burton-on-Trent, DE14 3HE

Printed and bound by
CPI Group (UK) Ltd, Croydon CR0 4YY

For my grandchildren
Josephine, Tom, Anna and Alex

Chapter One

'No one is dressed like a daffodil'

They were both in bed, almost asleep – Mary clutching a bundle of bedclothes 'in case I need to turn around', Hetty pulling the bedclothes from the other side. Then there was me, the youngest, aged six, sleeping in the middle, unable to move, almost strangled by the tight bedcovers.

The lamp outside our window shone through the crack between the flowery curtains and into the tiny bedroom I shared with my sisters: Hetty, aged eleven, and Mary, aged nine. The walls of our bedroom were painted white and the floor was covered with a pink-and-blue linoleum that matched the curtains. Beside the bed was a single, dark wooden wardrobe and on the other side there was a small dressing table and a tiny chest of drawers.

Although our bedroom was cosy, there was no heating, and in the winter we made sure we always got into bed quickly to keep warm. Climbing out of the bed, on the other hand, proved a bit more of a challenge – as sharing the bed with my sisters meant it was my bad luck to have to sleep in the middle.

Knowing this particular day was going to be special, even before opening my eyes, I carefully crawled to the bottom of the bed and managed to get out without disturbing them. It was still grey outside and there was a gentle breeze.

'What are you doing up already, Kitty?' Mum called from the other bedroom. 'It's only four o'clock – get back to bed!' Grudgingly, I returned to the end of the bed, sitting bolt upright, until I heard Mum's familiar call: 'Who's ready for a cup of tea?' She'd just returned from her early morning cleaning job; Dad was already at work and would return in the early afternoon. Tea? Tea? I wasn't interested in tea, having been waiting for months for this special outing.

'Shut up, all of you – I'm trying to sleep!' Hetty shouted as she turned on her side, pulling all the covers off Mary, who had taken advantage of the space I'd left, and was now sleeping next to her.

'What are you doing? I'm freezing – I hate you!' shouted Mary, as she tugged at the bedcovers from the other side, simultaneously prodding Hetty's back with her elbow.

'I don't care and I hate you!' Hetty replied.

'If you two don't stop, you won't be going out!' Mum shouted. This was the first argument of the day, but there was nothing unusual about it. Outside the flat and at school, Hetty and Mary were very protective of each other. All three of us had planned to meet up with Hetty's friends at the tram stop at eight o'clock that morning, but with Hetty and Mary still arguing, the likelihood of this happening was dwindling.

Leaving them to it, I wandered into the kitchen where Mum had prepared a huge plate of thick, hot buttered toast, which she'd placed on top of the green-and-white gingham tablecloth. Even the sight and smell of the toast couldn't tempt me. I was far too excited.

I could see through the kitchen door that Mary was now dressed and gazing into the dressing table mirror, admiring her curly blonde hair. I was willing her to hurry up, but at the same time admiring her prettiness and wishing my hair was just like hers.

'How much longer will they be?' I asked Mum.

'Try to be patient – otherwise they might not take you,' she said, patting my head.

'I don't want to go and meet up with Hetty's stuck-up friends anyway!' shouted Mary from the bedroom.

Hetty had, by this time, also managed to drag herself out of bed and was now ready to leave. Having been awake since four o'clock, I felt that my sisters were deliberately trying to make me wait longer.

'Hurry up, you two. I've got enough work to do without you slowing me down. Now get your coats on and make sure you take care of Kitty,' Mum called.

Reluctantly, Mary grabbed hold of my arm as we walked to our front door. Mum stopped fussing and gave us each a paper bag containing sandwiches for our lunch. She also handed Hetty a bag of clothes.

'If you don't stop jumping about, I'm not taking you,' said Hetty to me. Being the eldest child in our family, Hetty always had the last say. Mum relied on her quite a lot, and we were never bullied or teased at school when she was around. Not having any idea where we were going that morning, I just felt happy to be going anywhere with my sisters and their friends.

'Don't let go of her hand,' Mum shouted to my sisters. I was wearing one of Mary's dresses which she'd outgrown, and looking very grown-up. The dress was pale blue, covered in tiny red flowers.

'Why is Kitty wearing my dress?' demanded Mary. 'It's my favourite.' Mum told me to ignore her, giving my hand a little squeeze. I gave Mary a curtsy and ran off, grinning.

We walked along the side road, where there was a small shop. This was known to us as the Sweet Shop, although it sold almost everything – groceries and newspapers, as well as sweets.

'Come on,' said Hetty. 'Mum's given us sixpence to spend. You can have two pennies each.' I was momentarily mesmerised by the colourful display of sweets, but my eyes were soon drawn to my favourites – bullseyes and liquorice sticks. 'Hurry up, we can't be late!' barked Hetty.

Little did we know how important this tiny shop would become to our family in the years to come. On the corner of the road was a pub Dad would escape to on a Saturday night for a beer with his friends and neighbours, after a heavy week cleaning the streets of the City of London. Wearing his best suit, he always looked so smart on this, his one night out. This small area was my world, where I was allowed to walk alone or meet up with my friends. These side streets were my playground and felt safe.

Eventually we reached the main road, busy with noisy traffic, including huge red trams leading to unknown places. It felt both exciting and frightening, so I clung onto Hetty's arm. Now that Mary was certain she was well out of Mum's view, she let go of my arm and walked on ahead of Hetty and me. We could see two girls waving to us.

'Look, there's Joan and Polly!' cried Hetty, wild with excitement. Polly ran towards me, smiling, and took hold of my hand. She was wearing a floral dress with a white frill around the bottom and she had a big white ribbon in her hair.

'You stay with me, Kitty. I'll take care of you,' she said, as we trailed behind everyone. Of all my sisters' friends, Polly was my favourite. She bent down to give me a hug and by the look in my sisters' eyes, it was clear they were glad to hand over my care to someone else. Polly was an only child and she loved to play mother to me.

We joined the long queue for our tram, which eventually came rattling noisily along the tracks in the road. Hetty held out her arm proudly to stop it and we all scrambled on.

'Let's all go upstairs so we'll get a good view!' shouted Hetty.

'Hurry along,' said the conductor, a tall thin man with a tired face. He had a smart peaked cap and wore an important-looking badge on his jacket. In his hand was a long strip of coloured tickets.

'Fares please!' he called out. We each paid our half-penny fare and in exchange were each given a tiny ticket. As we climbed up the stairs, I was still wondering where we were going but really didn't care too much. The journey was long but as we'd managed to get seats at the front, we just sat entranced by the amazing busyness of London. People were running in all directions, everyone seeming to be in such a hurry, and we passed many tall buildings. Finally, Polly stood up. We all jumped off. She seemed very confident.

'We've a bit of a walk ahead of us,' Polly said as she looked down at me, smiling and squeezing my hand. She always made me feel special. The next thing I noticed was an enormous golden statue, shining in the sun.

'That's Queen Victoria's husband, Albert,' said Hetty, which made me wonder how you could have a husband made of gold.

Mary was still walking on ahead, pretending not to be with us.

Suddenly, what looked like a palace appeared in front of us. It was the Royal Albert Hall. We walked round and round this circular building, while Polly tried to find the right entrance. Sensing we were lost, a woman in a smart uniform asked if she could help us.

'You children need to go to Entrance D and get changed. You don't need to buy tickets as you're going to be part of the show.' Where was Entrance D? What show was she talking about?

'Behave yourself and keep close to me,' Hetty said, as she grabbed my arm and pulled me towards her.

The year was 1936 and we'd come to the Royal Albert Hall to take part in a fancy-dress competition. The venue was full of families, eager for their children to win. We finally found our entrance, which was packed with children, pushing and shoving. Two young women in red-and-gold uniforms were trying unsuccessfully to create some order. Suddenly, a giant of a man appeared. He was wearing a blue suit covered with gold braid, and a peaked cap.

'Quiet!' he shouted. 'You will form a queue or all get out.' There was silence. An orderly queue was quickly formed, and we made our way to what we were told was the back of the stage and the dressing rooms. Here chaos reigned – with laughing, screaming, enthusiastic children all hoping to win a competition. It was so hot in that dressing room that I was beginning to wonder if I wanted to stay after all. Too late! Hetty grabbed my arm.

'Take off your coat. Let's get you ready,' she said. Ready for what? I still didn't know what this was all about, but I was glad to shed some clothes at last. Coats, hats, scarves and socks were strewn everywhere. Everyone was laughing and enjoying the moment and fighting for space.

'Anyone seen a brown lace-up shoe?' someone shouted. My shoes remained firmly on my feet.

From the bag Mum had given her, Hetty pulled out a yellow-and-green outfit.

'What is it? What's that supposed to be?'

'It's a daffodil, stupid. Try to remember if you're asked,' said Hetty. Mum had sent me to the Royal Albert Hall with a daffodil costume.

Neither Hetty nor Mary had any clothes to change into, so it looked to me as though it was just Polly and I who were taking to the stage. Polly wore her mother's hat and shuffled about in high-heeled shoes, but I wasn't sure what she was supposed to be. Both boys and girls were competing, the boys dressed mainly as animals or monsters. I spotted Alfie Mack, who lived in our block of flats. He was supposed to be a lion and kept flicking his tail in my face.

'Leave her alone or I'll pull your tail off,' Hetty warned him.

'Just try!' retorted Alfie.

None of the boys seemed particularly interested in the competition. They just enjoyed grunting, pretending to be animals. Backstage, everyone was having great fun, trying to guess what we were supposed to be. Before I could object, Hetty had slipped yellow-and-green fabric over my head and with a sharp tug pulled my arms through the holes.

We were then told to line up, march up a few steps and walk across the stage, where we had to parade in front of three women and two men who were taking notes. Someone whispered that these were the judges. To me, they looked very stern and old. All the other girls looked beautiful in their outfits and this made me feel a little uncomfortable.

'No one is dressed like a daffodil,' I complained to Hetty.

'Oh, stop moaning and hold your head high. It's good that no one else is a flower,' she replied.

'Well, I don't think it's good. I feel stupid,' I muttered.

'You look wonderful,' Polly said, trying to reassure me. Not wanting to belittle Mum's efforts, I just gritted my teeth and carried on. We shuffled across the stage and then we all assembled back in the dressing room. We felt more relaxed now. Someone was calling out numbers. It was of no interest to me – I was beginning to enjoy myself.

'103! Will ticket number 103 please come to the stage?' There was an urgency in the announcement. 'Will the child with number 103 come to the stage immediately?' The voice sounded even more impatient and everyone backstage started panicking and looking for this number. I didn't know what was going on, and in any case I was far too happy laughing and chatting to my new friends to pay any attention to the announcement. All I knew, from listening to the others, was that we were taking part in a fancy-dress competition for the Girls' Life Brigade. Although I felt awkward dressed as a daffodil, just being in the Royal Albert Hall and playing a part in this huge extravaganza felt special.

Hetty told me that Mum, with a little bit of help from her, had been working on my costume in every spare minute she could find. The idea had come to her when she saw one lonely daffodil pushing its way up through the soil in a neighbour's flowerpot. Its tall green shoot looked full of promise. The brave little flower had flourished in a world of bricks and concrete. We already had an old green school jumper and green stockings; all Mum had to buy was some yellow crêpe paper. Looking at my costume, I could see the care Mum had taken.

'Move your arms around as if you're in a breeze,' Hetty snapped.

Just as I was beginning to imagine what an impressive daffodil I might be, a hand was on my shoulder and I was pushed back onto the stage by a tall, excited woman with glasses perched on the end of her nose and her hair piled high on her head.

'Here she is!' she screeched, pointing to a large number tied onto my outfit. The number was 103. It was me they were looking for. I'd been chosen as one of the finalists out of hundreds of children, and was now being pushed onto the stage to join eight other finalists, much older than me. Why me? Looking at the lovely costumes the bigger girls were wearing, I thought there must be some mistake. Hetty had her hands on her cheeks, her mouth wide open.

We had to stand in front of the five judges who were looking us up and down. At that moment, panic set in. I shouldn't even have been at the Royal Albert Hall, being far too young to be a member of the Girls' Life Brigade. I was only there because my two older sisters were members.

The other finalists were all smiling and preening themselves. Some of them were even wearing make-up and their costumes all seemed very sophisticated. There was a princess with a sparkling crown on her head, and a fairy complete with wings, a halo and a wand. Standing at the end of the line, having been pushed on at the last moment, I was half the age and size of the others. I began to feel scared and looked around for Polly, but she was nowhere to be seen.

Then a tall woman, wearing a long red dress and a tiny black hat and with very scarlet lips, began to walk behind us. She was holding a board with the word 'applause' written on it. I didn't see her at first but could hear the audience responding with clapping and cheering. As she walked behind each child, she held the board up high. The princess received a loud applause and gave a sweet little curtsy in response. As the woman moved along the line towards me, I began to feel alarmed. Becoming aware that she was holding the board up behind me, I looked down to the front of the audience and there, to my utter joy, I saw Dad. He looked so happy and was waving his cap high in the air to catch my attention. I waved back, jumping up and down and blowing him kisses with both hands. The entire audience stood up and there was huge applause. They thought the kisses were for them. This simple act won the hearts of the crowd. Having received the loudest applause, I had won the competition.

Hetty ran towards me and kissed and hugged me. Polly, with her mother's hat on one side of her head and clasping the high-heeled shoes in her hands, also kissed me, but my eyes were only for Dad. He must have taken the day off work just to be there for me, and he would now have to work on his day off, as he certainly couldn't afford to lose a day's pay. I'd won the silver cup for the South London Girls' Life

Brigade. One of the judges tied a wide green-and-gold sash across my chest, but all that mattered to me was that I'd made Dad so happy.

Chapter Two

Happy families

Life was good. Although very poor, we were a happy family with many friends. Home was a two-bedroom flat in Camberwell, South London, set in a block with forty other families. It was a small, comfortable flat and all of us in the building knew and trusted one another. We always left our front door key hanging on a piece of string just behind the letter box so neighbours could let themselves in. We were also free to come and go in and out of our friends' homes at any time. To me, the whole block was just like one big family. The boys would play football together in our courtyard, and Mum would remark on how polite they were when they apologised for kicking their football too near her window. Two of these boys would later become notorious gangsters.

I shared a bedroom with my sisters, and it overlooked a grassy area, which the council cut twice a year and which was only accessible by climbing out of the window. This would become important in our lives a few years later. My sisters and I sometimes risked climbing out, as this grass was the only bit of green nearby and we could pretend we were having a picnic, propping our dolls up against the wall and feeding them with imaginary food. My dolls' names were Betsy and Florence. Betsy didn't have any hair and Florence had blonde hair that stuck up like a toothbrush. We would sit outside for hours, playing on that patch of grass. 'You'll catch your death of cold sitting out there!' Mum would shout from the window, while handing us thick slices of bread and dripping, sprinkled with salt and pepper.

My best friends were Jean and Joan and when we weren't at school, we'd play together in the courtyard. Joan had her own doll and doll's pram. It was a beautiful pram, with a bright blue shiny body, a black shade that could go up or down, and silk covers. I loved pushing it around the courtyard, pretending it was mine, while knowing we'd never have enough money for me to own a pram myself. In return, Joan would borrow my skipping rope. We'd tie one end of the rope onto the washing pole and one of us would turn the free end, allowing the other to skip. We were never bored. One of the games we played was 'Knocking Down Ginger', which wasn't popular with the neighbours. We'd knock on people's doors and then hide as best we could, while still being able to keep an eye on the reaction of whoever opened their front door to find no one there. We thought it was a great game, but for obvious reasons, we couldn't play it too often.

Joan was a pretty girl, with long, dark, shiny hair. She was always beautifully dressed in clothes that had been bought just for her, an experience unknown to me. Despite this, I was never envious of her since, being an only child, she always seemed lonely. No matter how much my sisters and I argued, they were always there for me.

The courtyard was small and as the boys' games were always more boisterous than ours, they were often in some kind of trouble. Windows would sometimes get broken or a ball would get tangled up in the washing hanging out to dry, but it never stopped the boys having fun. 'OK, come on, who was it?' Mum would shout, when a window was smashed, most of the boys having run off. Alfie would stand by, looking innocent. 'Don't know, Mrs Baxter, ain't us, we don't know nuffink about it,' he'd say as he strolled away.

As we lived on the ground floor, we often heard Mum calling from our window, 'Mind my windows' or 'Mind my washing', to the boys playing football at the other end of the courtyard. It was in this courtyard that we sometimes exchanged our comics, the *Beano* or the *Dandy*. When we heard the words 'Tea's ready', everyone would look up to see who was calling. This was my world and I was happy with it.

Mum came from a big family. She had eleven brothers and sisters, some of whom had children of their own. No one ever understood the reason why, but we children didn't know anything about Dad's family. Nan and Grandad on Mum's side were very special to me and we saw them regularly, at least once a week. Nan was totally blind – she'd had a problem with her eyes when she was about fifty years old, and this gradually led to her losing her eyesight completely. There was no National Health Service in those days, so an operation to save her sight was out of the question, as it would have been far too expensive. Whenever anyone referred to her eyesight, Nan would say, 'Worse things happen at sea.' Never having been on a boat, I didn't argue with her about that. Nan never complained about her blindness and always had a penny in her apron pocket for me whenever we met. 'Don't tell anyone, it's only for you,' she'd say, as she fumbled for the coin. I knew she gave a penny to all of us: she loved us all and wouldn't dream of treating us differently.

Nan's disability taught me from a young age how and when to help blind people; I knew to pause before a step and walk close to the wall when we were out, so she felt safe. Grandad took great care of Nan. I liked to watch him do little things, like making her cups of tea and helping her by taking her small hand in his huge, work-worn ones, and gently guiding her tiny fingers through the handle of a cup. Grandad was a dock worker at Surrey Docks, but he was always in and out of work, as the dockers had to fight for the employment that was only available when the ships came in from abroad. To me, Grandad seemed a big strong man, a man of few words, who enjoyed his pint on a Saturday night, but his care for Nan was touching.

During our six-week school holiday, we'd go hop-picking in Kent and it was the highlight of our year. Hop-picking was the working person's holiday and everyone got excited as the season drew near. Mrs Rumble, our next-door neighbour, would lend us her special heavy cooking pans and some extra blankets to take with us.

'Here you are, love, some bits to help you out. You have a nice time. I'll keep an eye on your flat,' she'd say to Mum.

Mrs Rumble lived alone, a widow without children. She was a large, jolly woman who always seemed to have a bad cough and had difficulty getting around – and for this reason, she never joined us on our hop-picking excursions. She was a good neighbour and Mum was always ready to shop for her if she couldn't get out. Mrs Rumble was almost an extension of our family, as were most of our neighbours.

Together with our neighbours, we'd go hop-picking at the same time and to the same place in Kent every year. Three families at a time would head off in a lorry, which throughout the year they'd clubbed together to hire. There was also a particular train just for hop-pickers, known as the Hop-Pickers' Special. Our family, together with one other family, travelled in a removal van owned by one of Dad's friends. The extra space allowed Mum to take her own Primus stove and extra blankets. It also saved on train fares, though we paid for petrol. We'd sing all the way to Kent – 'Maybe it's Because I'm a Londoner' and 'We Are the Camberwell Girls'.

When we arrived, each family was allotted a small hut that was filled with masses of dry straw. The first job for us children was to fill our pillowcases with straw, and we had a great time throwing it everywhere. Then we'd spread a blanket over the rest of the straw on the floor or, if we were lucky, on raised wooden slats. Beds made, we'd then set about putting up our folding table and chairs outside the hut to make our dining area. All the mums worked hard making the huts cosy, although they were only just big enough to sleep in. The huts were made of corrugated iron sheets. They had earth floors and no doors and were lit by paraffin lamps.

After a busy day picking hops, from seven in the morning until dusk, we'd sit outside our huts beside a log fire that one of our parents had prepared earlier that day. Mum cooked on her little camping stove, while other families made small fires from twigs gathered in the woods.

Our food came mainly from a small shop on site. Meals consisted mostly of soup, made from fresh vegetables picked from local farms – the stewing pot simmering day and night. With this, we ate freshly baked bread from the local baker. Children were also allowed to pick berries from the hedges – it was great fun despite the stinging nettles and brambles – and once the berries were covered in condensed milk, they made a delicious dessert. Years later, the taste of condensed milk would always take me straight back to those heady hop-picking days.

Each family would stay in Kent for about four weeks, but the men usually returned home after a week to get back to their proper jobs. We managed to earn as much in one week's hop-picking as the men earned in four weeks doing their regular work. But hop-picking was seasonal and the men had to make sure they didn't lose their jobs.

Once a week, Mum would produce a small tin bath in which we children would stand and sponge each other down. We were supposed to take it in turns to bring water from a nearby communal tap, but when it was Mary's turn to fetch water, she always used to think up increasingly improbable excuses for not being able to get it. We'd heat the water up on our little stove before using it. Funnily enough, although Mary always seemed to evade the process of collecting the water, she had an uncanny ability to be the first in it.

Our toilet was a DIY affair, just a hole in the ground. We used to wander off with a shovel, dig a hole, do whatever we had to do and fill the hole with earth. It was a standing joke when anyone picked up the shovel. 'Have a good time!' everyone would shout. I didn't wander too far. I was happy to have them in my sight, not realising they could see me.

Hop-picking was hard work and our living conditions were basic, but it was one of my favourite times of the year. The freedom we had to explore the countryside and to smell the country air was in stark contrast to our London lives, which were full of the hustle and bustle of the city. These were the only holidays we knew and they were magical days when, for a short time, we were together.

Only just eclipsing our treasured hop-picking holidays was Christmas, when the whole family would gather at Nan's house in South Bermondsey for a special lunch.

On Christmas Eve, three pillowcases were placed at the end of the bed and, as if by magic, a new colouring book and crayons appeared in mine the next morning.

'Well, what have you got?' Hetty asked. In her pillowcase were some coloured embroidery silks, along with knitting wool and needles. Hetty was delighted – she loved to knit and sew. Mary had writing pads and pencils. These presents kept us busy most of the day. In my pillowcase, there was also a length of red ribbon for my hair, and a tangerine. We felt so happy and lucky – what more could we want? Little did we know then that tangerines, oranges, bananas and any imported fruit or food would soon be unavailable for many years.

Early on Christmas morning, we'd set about making decorations from strips of newspaper and a jar of paste Mum had made from flour and water. 'Don't use all the newspaper – we need to save some for the toilet,' Mum would say. No one could afford toilet rolls, so neat little squares of newspaper with string threaded through them would hang in the toilet for our use.

Hanging our paper decorations around the room, Mum gave a contented sigh and said, 'Now that looks properly like Christmas!' as last week's news looked down on us.

We always started Christmas Day with masses of tasty, hot buttered toast from thickly sliced crusty bread, but before we left for Nan's house, a small tin bath appeared. 'Come on then, who wants to be the first?' Mum asked. We all wanted to be first while the water was clean, but we had to bath one at a time as the bath was only big enough for one person. The water was normally heated in a stone copper in the kitchen, but as it was Christmas Day and we were in a hurry, saucepans of hot water from the cooker were the order of the day.

No matter what the weather was like, Christmas always promised to be a fun day and we were always full of excitement as we set off, presents in hand. Christmas Day was also the day for new shoes and socks, which we knew would have to last for most of the following year.

Nan always greeted us with outstretched hands and showered us with hugs and kisses.

'Hello, Nan, it's Kitty,' I'd say, so that she had some idea who was kissing her.

'I know,' she'd reply to make me feel special. She would be wearing a new flowery apron, her grey hair fastened back with a clip and a tiny curl hanging each side of her wrinkled face.

Every year, Mum and Dad would have put money aside each week so that we could contribute to the cost of the food and, to my astonishment, even though she couldn't see what she was doing, before we arrived Nan would have prepared all the vegetables for the meal, just by feeling her way through the task. Even the runner beans were sliced so finely that a machine could not have produced a better result. We would all sit at the table together and eat turkey, roast potatoes and all the trimmings, followed by a wobbly strawberry jelly and home-made mince pies. After lunch, Nan would wash the dishes.

'No, no, you sit down, it's my turn to wash up today,' Nan would insist. This was a big task, with so many plates and pieces of cutlery. She would have to feel her way round each item to know if it was clean and the result was always spotless, despite her blindness. Nan was a clever, independent woman, able to do so many things without her sight.

Once everything had been put away, Nan and Grandad would have 'forty winks', as they called it. While they were sleeping, we'd arrange a little area for our stage. Each child would have prepared a song or dance: this was our Christmas entertainment as, at that time, there was no television. Nan did, however, have a gramophone which was wound up using a little handle on the side. It played vinyl records and we each had a little song which we sang every Christmas Day. My song began 'I'm going to lock my heart and throw away the key', which I sang while holding a heavy key in my hand. Everyone laughed and ducked as the key was thrown over my shoulder. This always brought such laughter even though everyone knew what to expect. We had many entertaining records – George Formby singing 'When I'm Cleaning Windows' and 'The Lambeth Walk' were among our favourites. As Hetty shouted, 'Oi! Come on, all in a line behind me!' we'd perform all the actions, including sticking our thumbs up in the air as we danced around the room.

At around eleven o'clock we'd say goodbye to Nan and Grandad and start the long walk home.

One Saturday, Dad took me out for a special treat. He must have finished work early as it was unusual for him not to be on the job at this time. He called me from the playground.

'Come on, Kitty. I'll take you out for an ice cream. Mum has a headache and needs a rest. Hetty will stay with her.'

'Can I bring Joan?' I asked, but Dad was already making his way up the road. 'Hurry up, Joan!' I called, inviting her along anyway. Joan's coat came flying over the balcony.

'Put this on or you'll catch your death,' yelled her mum. Even though it was a warm day, Joan an only child was always over-fussed.

It was quite a long walk to the ice cream shop in East Lane, which was our local marketplace. The sun was shining and there was a warm breeze. Rossi's ice cream was a special treat, with twenty different flavours to choose from, and we had to take our time. 'Come on, luv, I ain't got all day – wot are you 'aving?' Mr Rossi spoke like a cockney but looked very Italian with his brown skin and big black moustache. It was hard to choose from so many colours but a decision was made and we walked away in a dreamlike state, licking our wonderful ice cream.

It felt as though you could buy anything you wanted in the market. All the stallholders would be shouting, 'Get your bargain here!' Every stall had something interesting to sell and we could have stayed in the market all day, so I didn't mind that Dad seemed to be lingering longer than usual, stopping at almost every stall. Joan and I skipped all along the way. Just being out with him was so special. But eventually the thrill of exploring the market came to an end as we started to make our way home.

As we approached our flats, I could see many of our neighbours leaning over their balconies, looking into the courtyard. I couldn't understand why they were smiling and waving at Dad. Mrs Rumble gave Dad a hug. 'Oh congratulations!' she said. Had he won the football pools that he studied every weekend? Dad always said, 'When I win the pools, it will be for you.' What was going on? Inside our kitchen was a different smell – not the usual smell of food but of disinfectant, a bit like the vapour rub that was smeared on our chests when we had colds.

'Wash your hands, Kitty, and then you can go into the bedroom to say hello to Mum,' Hetty said. After washing my hands, using the small enamel bowl in the kitchen sink, I walked into the bedroom where Mum was sitting up in bed, a huge smile on her red, shiny face. I was pleased to see that she no longer had a headache, but my attention was drawn to the missing drawer from the large chest of drawers that stood in the corner of the room. Looking more closely, I saw it was now beside Mum's bed, propped up on two chairs with a soft white blanket inside.

'Come round, I've something to show you,' said Mum softly. She pointed to the drawer. Peering inside, I couldn't believe my eyes. Peeking out from under the blanket was a baby.

'Who does it belong to?' I asked. Mum smiled.

'Shush,' she said, putting her finger to her lips. 'This is William, your new baby brother. We've named him after Dad but we'll call him Billy. Now go and have your tea.'

'I've made you a salmon and shrimp paste sandwich. Mum wants to get some sleep,' Hetty said, trying to prise me away from all the excitement.

Reluctantly, I returned to the kitchen, wondering why Mum needed sleep. Dad had the biggest smile on his face and he seemed to have got taller, walking with his shoulders back and head held high. The baby was Billy, my new brother and the first son for Dad after three daughters. Later that evening, amidst all the fuss, Mum allowed me to hold Billy, providing I sat down. I sat like a statue, afraid to move a muscle, until my neck began to feel stiff and I had to hand him back. His tiny screwed-up face was adorable and he had a sweet scent, one I'd never smelt before. He put his tiny hand round my finger and I couldn't wait to tell Joan that I now had a real baby to push around in a pram, but that she could still borrow my skipping rope.

The next day, Mum was up and about as usual and back to work at her job. She worked for the War Office as a cleaner from five to eight in the morning and was back home in time to see us off to school. She then returned to work from five to eight in the evening. While Mum was working, Hetty took care of Billy, changing his nappy and bathing him. This system worked well and meant we were able to be together in the evening and at bedtime.

'When can I hold him again?' I repeatedly implored Hetty, and was allowed to do so for a short while every night before going to bed, rocking him gently and singing him a little song. Before long, Mary too was allowed to help with some of the duties involved in looking after Billy. She and Hetty would take it in turns to bath him and put him in his bed.

'Come on, Kitty, time for his powder,' said Hetty and I was allowed to gently powder him dry.

Around this time, great changes were also taking place in our country and we had a new king, George VI. We were thrilled because our new king had two little girls, Elizabeth and Margaret, who were about the same age as Hetty and me.

In May of 1937, huge street parties took place all over the country for the king's coronation, with tables stretching from one end of the street to the other. In our street alone, the table must have seated about a hundred children. Mum and Dad came along with Nan and Grandad, and Billy in his pram. Mum looked so fashionable in her ankle-length coat with a fake-fur collar and a tiny cloche hat. I sat next to a boy who was wearing a jacket made from a Union Jack. I felt a little envious but it didn't spoil the fun. Everyone in our block of flats made a contribution to the event and beneath the sweltering sun, we devoured masses of food which included my favourites – jam scones with real cream, and even fizzy lemonade. We were each given a little flag to wave, and flags and bunting hung from every window. The whole country was celebrating, but we would all go through great turmoil before we would ever see another street party.

Billy grew to be a beautiful boy with long blond curls, which, despite all our efforts to get her to change her mind, Mum refused to have cut. She would spend a long time every morning curling his hair round her fingers in ringlets, when all he wanted to do was go out and play. With his curls, poor Billy looked like a little girl and we'd tease him and call him Jessie, but he never realised we were laughing at his hair. One day, when Billy was about four years old, Dad took him out for a walk and to Mum's horror, they arrived back home with Dad carrying all Billy's curls in a paper bag. At last Billy, who was growing into a rough-and-tumble little boy, looked like his friends.

'Oh no, what have you done to him?' Mum cried. My sisters and I laughed hysterically.

'Who's this handsome boy?' Hetty teased him.

Billy was pleased to be rid of his curls and couldn't wait to run out, an old ball tucked under his arm, with his best friend, also named Billy – a large lad we referred to as Big Billy. Although the youngest and smallest, brother Billy was always the goalkeeper. The boys made goalposts using two washing poles in the yard. Billy was so small you could have got two buses in the space either side of him, but he did his best to defend his area.

Billy now began to insist on being called Bill, like his dad, but with three older sisters, he had a tough time getting his own way. He always remained Billy to us. The haircut, which seemed to make Billy grow up overnight, had other repercussions. He refused to wear his nightwear, an old dress of mine that I'd outgrown.

'Well, that's not a problem. I can cut the dress in half, sew up the middle of the bottom half and make you a lovely pair of pyjamas,' said Mum, ever one for making something go a long way.

'You can sew as much as you like. I'm never wearing them again!' said Billy, throwing the dress across the room. Thereafter, he insisted on sleeping in his vest and pants. Although we continued to tease Billy, we noticed he was beginning to stand his own ground and fight back. He was the only boy in the family, but we never spoilt him.

Chapter Three

Ways with water

There was no question in our family about who'd be the first to use the bathroom, as we simply didn't have one. We just took it in turns to wash in the enamel bowl kept in the kitchen sink. Above the sink there was only a cold-water tap, so a small saucepan was kept on the gas stove with warm water in it for our daily washing needs. Our bath was under a huge wooden flap in the kitchen, which also served as our kitchen table.

Once a week, Mum would heat the water in a copper next to the bath. The copper was our main water heater: it was like a very big, deep bucket without a handle, encased in stone. Although it was

53

called a copper, the bucket itself was made of cast iron. The bucket had to be filled and emptied using a saucepan, as there was no tap attached to it. The water was heated by a fire which was fuelled by small sticks and coal in an opening at the bottom. The copper had a wooden lid to keep the water clean and hot while it was heating up. When the water was hot enough, Mum would scoop it out and gradually fill the bath. 'Who's going to be first?' Mum would call out from the kitchen. We all kept silent. The choice was – did we go first and get a dry towel, or wait until the kitchen had warmed up?

The copper was also used for our weekly laundry. Mum would boil our white sheets in it, using wooden tongs to agitate the water and lift the sheets out when they were clean. The soapy water that remained in our bath was used to wash all our coloured clothes. Finally, any remaining water was used to scrub the linoleum floors with the same carbolic soap that we'd used for bathing and washing our clothes.

'Put all your dirty clothes in the bath,' said Mum after we'd finished bathing. Then out would come

Mum's scrubbing board and the clothes would be rubbed up and down the board in the bath, before being tossed into clean water in the sink.

The sheets and clothes were then all carefully folded and put through a mangle, which was housed just outside the kitchen in a small passage that led to the front door. A mangle was a contraption about five feet high, with a big handle at the side and two large wooden rollers. Mum would feed the washing through the rollers by turning the handle, and the rollers would squeeze out most of the excess water into a bucket placed underneath. There was a screw at the top of the mangle to adjust the rollers according to the thickness of the fabric.

'Who's going to turn the handle for me?' Mum would call out. At that point we'd all disappear. Once the mangle had done its work, Mum would hang the washing out in the courtyard to finish drying. Terry-towelling nappies would often hang around everywhere. Disposable nappies didn't exist, nor did washing machines or tumble dryers. Women would spend almost all of the day washing, ironing, cleaning and cooking and had very little time for themselves.

Sometimes, if Mum was too busy for this long bath routine, and if she could afford it, she'd send us to the public baths near Camberwell Green. Manor Place Baths was a large, imposing building, about a twenty-minute walk away. We felt proud to be walking up the stone steps to gain entry. I could barely reach the ticket office but felt very grown-up to have my own bathroom. For three pennies you could get a hot bath with a very itchy towel included in the price. It was a special treat to go to the baths, and for us to each have our own towel, even if it was itchy! Once we'd paid our money, we were each given a numbered ticket, a small amount of soap and a towel, and we'd sit in the waiting room listening out for the call.

'Next, second!' 'Second' meant second class. Six pennies would buy a first-class ticket, which meant that the towel would be a lot softer and the bath would have more water in it. Either way, a bathroom would be allocated just for you, except that it was nothing like a conventional bathroom. It was a very small cubicle containing only a bath and a handrail. The flow of the water was controlled by the attendant outside the cubicle. If you needed more hot or cold water, you'd simply shout out the number of your cubicle followed by a request for either hot or cold. If you stayed in the bath too long, the attendant would drain out the water, using the controls outside your bathroom.

'What number are you in? Are you nearly finished?' Hetty would call out.

'Yeah, just getting dressed, see you outside in a few minutes!' I'd reply.

One way or another, either using the copper or going to Manor Place, Mum made certain we all had a bath and a hair wash once a week.

Fridges and freezers were other appliances that did not exist in those days, at least not for us. We put our milk and other perishables out on the windowsill to keep them cool, although this didn't always work.

'Ugh, this milk is all lumpy!' Billy would often complain.

'Just give it a good stir,' would be Mum's stock response.

As the NHS didn't exist then either, Mum would pay one penny a week to the Hospital Saving Association, an organisation that would help if you had to visit a doctor or hospital. There were many times when Mum couldn't afford the penny for that week, and we had to be very quiet and pretend we weren't at home when the man called to collect the money. 'Shush! Don't make a sound!' Mum would say, as we climbed onto a chair to peek out of the window and see who was at the door.

We would all breathe a sigh of relief when we heard the money collector's footsteps grow fainter as he walked away. However, we rarely needed to visit a doctor. A spoonful of syrup of figs soon made us feel better, even if the taste was vile! A tin of Vaseline was also always at hand to soothe all cuts and grazes, and that completed our medicine cabinet.

When she wasn't at work, most of Mum's day was taken up with cooking and cleaning, but we all had our own jobs to do at home. Like all of us, Billy had his daily chore, tidying up the comics – we were allowed one comic a week each, which we'd swap with our friends. My job was to get down on my hands and knees to scour the front porch with a scrubbing brush. I took great pride in doing this and there was always praise from the neighbours.

'That looks so wonderful,' they'd say as they passed. 'Oh, you're a good girl,' our neighbour Mrs Rumble, who shared our porch, would say, so she got her area scrubbed every week for free. I was glad to do this for her, as she'd always give me a sweet for my trouble.

Mary had the ironing to do but refused to iron Hetty's clothes. The iron was warmed up on the gas stove and it had to be held with a cloth while it was being used. It doubled up as a doorstop when not in use. Mary often wormed her way out of jobs, petulantly tossing her curls in the air with the back of her hand.

Hetty did the shopping at our local shop, the Sweet Shop, on the corner of the road. This was run by two elderly women who allowed us to borrow money known as 'tick', and pay later. Their names were Miss Right and Miss White and they were angry if you forgot who was who and called them by the wrong name. They would bustle about in the little shop, which had two counters. One side had fresh food like ham, butter and cheese – which was always cut with a wire slicer so that you could buy as much as you could afford – and the counter opposite had tinned food and the most amazing jars of sweets and chocolates, together with cigarettes. Hetty knew the thin woman was Miss Right, and the two women loved her for always remembering their names. For this reason, they let her buy food on tick. Hetty would also sweep out the shop at closing time for extra food, and of course, this delighted Mum. This little shop would soon become our lifeline.

Chapter Four

Birthday surprise

'Happy birthday to you! Happy birthday to you!'
Excited, I opened my eyes. It was my ninth birthday,
1st September 1939. Mum walked into the bedroom
carrying a parcel, wrapped in newspaper and tied
with red ribbon. Billy started to wake up. Mum
gently shook my shoulder, putting her fingers to her
lips, and said, 'Shush, don't wake the others. I've
something for you.'

Scrambling over Hetty who was fast asleep, I got
out of bed.

'What have you got?' Billy asked, rubbing his eyes.
But not wanting to share the moment even with Billy,
I left the bedroom and went into our cosy kitchen

to sit on a stool. A cloth covered the table, on which stood a teapot covered with a blue-and-white striped knitted tea cosy and four mugs waiting to be filled with hot, steaming tea.

Mum had the wireless on, which was unusual so early in the morning. I began opening my parcel. It was just Mum and me at that moment, in what was normally a very crowded kitchen in the hub of our small flat. She stood over me, smiling. She'd rushed home from her office cleaning job, wanting to be back before anyone was up. I'd been concerned about Mum, as she'd been looking so worried lately and both Mum and Dad listened to the nine o'clock news intensely every night on the wireless. What was going on? I opened my special parcel slowly, savouring the moment. Inside was something soft – a pair of new pyjamas.

'Oh, Mum, they're wonderful! New pyjamas!' I'd never had new pyjamas in my entire life. They were white with little pink flowers. I couldn't help remembering that Mum had once had a tablecloth like that. But they were so pretty and all my own. All my other clothes had originally belonged to either Hetty or Mary. In the parcel there were also two new pairs of socks and two new pairs of knickers. And lying between the clothes was a tiny doll, about three inches tall, made of a kind of plastic called celluloid. She even had arms and legs that could move, and yellow hair painted onto her shiny head. She needed new clothes so I gently wrapped a lace-edged handkerchief around her, a cherished Christmas present from Nan. I put her on the windowsill hidden behind the curtains until school. I also carefully placed my folded new pyjamas next to her. Mum was beaming. As I put my arms around her, my cheek touched her hot, red face and her wisps of grey hair. It was a wonderful moment for both of us.

Mum was the boss in our family. We never argued with her. Just one look was enough to stop us fighting, and with three girls close in age there was always plenty to argue about. If the look didn't work, the words 'I'll tell your father' were used as a threat. Dad would just wink and grin but it was still enough. Peace would reign again, at least until the next row. But, despite our arguments, we were always very loyal to one another.

I went back to the bedroom and clambered over Billy, who'd fallen asleep again, to get my clothes ready for school. He didn't move and neither did my two sisters, who were sharing the same bed but at the opposite end. We also shared a single wardrobe. Hetty had one side and Mary the other. My clothes were somewhere in the middle. Even our dressing table had a line drawn down the middle to mark out whose side belonged to whom. Mary had a tiny old block of mascara for her eyelashes, which her friend had given her. She kept this on her side of the dressing table and twice a day she would examine it to see if there was any evidence of moisture, which would have indicated that someone else had used it. If this happened, Hetty was in big trouble. Hetty and Mary were very competitive and there was always a shouting match between them if any item happened to find its way to the wrong side of the line. Life was never boring. Billy and I were not interested in these matters.

By this time we had another addition to our family – another boy, Charlie. Our new baby slept in Mum and Dad's room in the top drawer of Mum's oak chest of drawers, as Billy had done when he was a baby. This made a comfortable cot. He'd been named after Mum's brother, Uncle Charlie, a soon-to-be hero at Dunkirk.

'Can I hold him?' I asked Mum, while giving him a little tickle under his chin and feeling certain he was giving me a smile in return. 'Look, he's smiling at me!' I said. He was wrapped in a soft white shawl and smelt so sweet. I loved taking care of him. He was always happy and contented, and had the same curly blond hair that Billy used to have. Charlie became *my* baby, as Hetty and Mary now had other interests, mainly clothes and boys.

Life had changed in other ways too. Hetty, Mary and I had all attended the same local school, which was a convenient short walk from home, but Mary had passed the eleven-plus exam and this had won her a place at a grammar school. Dad was thrilled and Mum borrowed the money for her uniform from our local moneylender, an elderly woman who lived nearby. In her navy gymslip, red blazer and straw hat, Mary looked so smart and I envied her a little.

Hetty and I also had to change schools and go to a church school, at the request of a local priest who would only baptise Charlie if we did so. Our new school was a long way from home, which meant we had to cross some main roads, so Mum had to take us with Billy and Charlie in tow, after getting back from her morning cleaning job. This made life more difficult for Mum but it was important to her to get Charlie baptised. We'd all been baptised and attended church every Sunday, and it was only now our priest insisted we went to a church school. It took us a long time to adjust and make new friends.

Dad worked in the City of London and was very proud of the work he did as a road sweeper. He would tell me about the famous street names and the famous landmarks. He began work at five in the morning but would return home in the afternoon. He was fussy about his appearance and always made sure he looked smart. Even as a road sweeper he wore clean, shiny shoes.

'Where are all the shoes?' he'd call out every evening, shoe brush in his hands. We had shiny shoes lined up in our hallway every morning, even if they had cardboard inside them to keep out the rain. As a child, Dad had no schooling and he was now teaching himself to read and write. Every evening, he'd shut himself in our sitting room with his books and pencils. These were strewn all over our dining table and no one else was allowed near it. This didn't matter, as we always ate in the kitchen anyway and visitors would usually sit there too. Sometimes Dad would call out to Mary to help him. She became his teacher. This meant she no longer had to help with the housework, which she thought was a very good bargain. We all had to be very quiet when they were working together, but with diligence and Mary's help, Dad gradually learnt to read and write. This was to prove essential over the next few years.

On this birthday, Dad appeared home earlier than normal. I rushed to show him my new pyjamas but when I saw him without his usual cheery smile and looking troubled, I began to wonder why and felt a little disappointed. Did he remember it was my birthday? He had a frown above his expressive, dark brown eyes. Why would he come home so early if it wasn't for me? What was going on? Was it to see Mum's brother

Charlie, again? Uncle Charlie had called by the day before in a brand-new uniform, looking so handsome. He was much younger than Dad, only nineteen. When he'd left, he hugged Dad who wished him good luck. What was going on? Why was everyone looking so serious? Even Mum was looking agitated and nothing normally ever fazed her. The news on the wireless seemed to be causing some concern. Something was making them look very troubled.

'Shush! Just be quiet. This is important,' Dad said, and I knew from the look on his face that it must be.

Mum and Dad moved closer to the wireless. Their anxious looks told me that something out of the ordinary was happening. I kept hearing the words 'war' and 'evacuation'.

'War? What does war mean?' I asked Dad.

'It's nothing for you to worry about,' he replied, patting my head. I was consoled by Dad's soothing words.

Then Mum was shouting out, 'Hetty, Mary, Kitty, you're all going on a trip to the countryside today.' I instantly forgot all about war and what was bothering Mum and Dad, believing that this was going to be my special trip, arranged just for me to celebrate my birthday. Little did I realise something sinister was happening in the world and this day, my ninth birthday, was not only going to be the last day of *my* beautiful, safe and secure childhood, but a day that would change the lives of millions of men, women and children. No one could ever have imagined what the future held.

We all looked at Mum in amazement. We couldn't believe what we were hearing. School had been very boring over the last few days. Instead of our usual lessons of reading and writing, we'd just been sitting at our desks playing games. Some children had even fallen asleep in class. It was a strange feeling, as if we were waiting for something to happen, and I wondered if it was this trip.

'We have to meet some other children,' Mum said. 'It's a trip for the whole school and just in case you stay overnight, each of you must take pyjamas, knickers and some socks. You'd better take your toothbrushes too.'

Never having been on a school trip before, I had no idea where we were going and felt anxious. Hetty and

Mary started to argue, as usual, about what clothes they were going to take, but Dad soon stopped all that by locking up the wardrobe.

'Just shut up you two, and help your mother,' Dad said sternly. He seldom got angry and I wondered what was making him so impatient.

Mum had three clean pillowcases ready to use as our travelling bags, as we didn't have suitcases. She'd threaded some string through each top to use as a handle. Finally the pillowcases were packed. Hetty also packed our toothbrushes and a small tin of pink toothpaste.

'As soon as you can, write and tell me where you are. Here's a stamped, addressed envelope, so take care not to lose it,' said Mum. Hetty tucked the envelope in her pocket for safety. What did Mum mean? Why didn't she know where we were going? Billy wanted to know why he didn't have a pillowcase, so Mum stuffed some old clothes into one and gave it to him so he didn't feel left out. Billy was still far too young to be going anywhere without Mum. Taking a look at my baby doll on the windowsill, I told her to be good and that I'd be back soon to play with her, not having any idea what a long time it would be before I'd see her again. All I knew was that we were going on holiday by train with all our friends. What could possibly be a more thrilling way to spend your ninth birthday?

At last, we were ready to make our way to school, where we were to meet up with all our friends. We all gathered in the playground. The whole school was in chaos. Some children were shouting with excitement, but some of the younger children were clinging onto their mothers and didn't seem happy to be going anywhere.

'Whatever you do, make certain you all stay together. I've put soap, flannel and the toothpaste in Hetty's bag and you will have to *share*,' Mum emphasised.

Both Mum and Dad came to school with us that day and brought Billy and Charlie with them to wave us off. The weather was good and so were our moods. Billy was happy enough holding his pillowcase and believing he was going to be part of the action, but when he realised he was staying behind he began to cry.

'Don't cry, Billy! I'll come back tomorrow and take you to the pictures to see *Snow White*,' I told him.

Now convinced it was going to be an overnight stay, I could feel the excitement in the air. We were missing sums that morning and we were all delighted at the fact. We were dressed in our best clothes and thought we looked very smart. Some children had even had their hair cut and carried a little suitcase instead of a pillowcase. After a lot of fussing around, our teacher Miss Giblin, got the children to line up. She was well spoken and always beautifully dressed. Today, she wore a green tailored suit and a tiny hat, finished off with smart brown shoes. We were ready to set off.

'Boys and girls, please keep together – I don't want to lose anyone,' she said. Each child was given a cardboard box with string through it. Inside was a small rubber mask called a gas mask and we laughed as we tried them on. They had a strange smell and they soon got misted up so we couldn't see out of them. We didn't leave them on for very long. They made us look like little pigs: the boys made oinking noises which made us girls laugh even more. Of course, we had no idea what they were for. We were just looking forward to our trip. We were then each handed a brown label to tie onto our coat. The label showed the name of our school and a number corresponding to the number of the coach we had to board.

Suddenly, the coaches arrived through the school gates. My heart skipped a beat. It was as if we were all going on a fantastic outing. The boys cheered as the coaches appeared. I clung onto Hetty's hand, while she held Mary with her other hand, trying to keep us all together as we'd promised Mum.

At last we were ready to set off. Everyone was excited. My best friend Joan had stayed at home and I felt sorry for her, thinking she'd miss out on all the fun. She really would have wanted to come with us but as she was an only child, her mum wasn't willing to let her go. Miss Giblin told us that the coach was going to take us to a train. I was even more certain now that it was going to be the best birthday ever and although I'd never been on a coach or train before, with Hetty on one side of me and Mary on the other, I felt quite safe.

We lined up ready to board our coach. There was a scramble as everyone rushed to get a window seat, but Hetty managed to get on first and save seats for us. The teachers were running around in all directions and taking care of the very small children. Among all the parents crowded in the playground, Mum and Dad were trying to follow us to wave goodbye. Searching frantically through the sea of faces, I eventually caught sight of Mum. To my horror, she was sobbing. She was holding Charlie and trying to hide her face by putting him in front of her, but it was too late – I'd already seen her crying. Why? Why? Why? Billy was clinging onto her skirt, looking as though he was also wondering why everyone was so sad. I suddenly wanted to get off the coach. What was wrong? What could possibly be upsetting her so much?

'I want to get off – Mum's crying,' I pleaded with Hetty. All the mums were in the front and the dads were at the back, so I couldn't see Dad. I turned to Hetty and Mary for reassurance, but they hadn't seen what I'd seen. It was too late. The shaky, rickety old coach had pulled out. I tried desperately to put the image of Mum's sad face to the back of my mind, but it continued to haunt me. Our teachers tried to get us to sing songs like 'Roll out the Barrel' and 'It's a Long Way to Tipperary' and most of us joined in. Alfie and Big Billy scrambled through their pillowcases looking for the sandwiches that their mothers had given them for the journey. Most of the children seemed happy but some remained very quiet and I wondered why, when we were all about to embark on such an enormous adventure.

After a while, we arrived at the railway station. There we saw many groups of soldiers who seemed to be heading off somewhere. I looked out for Uncle Charlie, but couldn't see him and thought it strange that there were hundreds of other children there too, all from different schools. They were waiting on the platform and looking just as confused as we felt. We all began to feel a bit apprehensive. Then a number of women appeared, wearing smart green hats with the initials WVS on them. They were from the Women's Voluntary Service, and one of their tasks was to help with the evacuation of women and children.

We were each given a tiny packet of cream crackers or rich tea biscuits, but were not given anything to drink in case we needed to go to the toilet. If this promised to be such a fun day out, why was no one looking excited any longer? We queued to get onto the train. Each carriage had about twelve seats but had to accommodate many more children, so lots had to sit on the floor. Some naughty-looking children were climbing everywhere. Two boys, about ten years old, climbed onto the luggage rack above my sisters and me. They were laughing and seemed to be enjoying the journey.

'Come on, let's sit up here,' said the lad with the biggest boots. I wasn't happy with their feet round my eyes, but Hetty came to the rescue: she grabbed their boots, pulled them off and hung onto them for the rest of the journey.

Suddenly, the train whistled. There was a huge puff of steam and off it went. There were no corridors on the train so, apart from my sisters, I was stuck in a small carriage with complete strangers. This was my special day and although I sometimes argued with my sisters, suddenly it felt very good to have them with me. The train journey seemed to take for ever. It had now started to rain a little and with the raindrops beating on the window, there was a slight chill in the air. We passed many tall buildings and traffic was everywhere. London seemed so busy. I must have fallen asleep, as I suddenly felt a gentle push on my shoulder.

'Wake up, wake up, Kitty! Here, have your cream crackers. You must be hungry by now,' said Hetty. Munching on my crackers, through the window I saw endless wide, open spaces and more green than I'd ever seen in my life. This was my first sight of the countryside, looking like a patchwork quilt of yellows, greens and browns. The trees were a mass of different shapes and sizes and there were cows lying down and standing everywhere. I tried to remember from my books whether this was a sign that it was going to rain, but as they were doing both, it didn't matter anyway. The views were breathtaking and better than anything I'd seen in any books. I fell in love with the countryside that day, but wondered where all the houses and the people were. Hetty told me that I'd slept for an hour. I now began to wish I'd listened to Mum before leaving London, as I needed the toilet. I tugged on Hetty's coat.

'I need the toilet,' I said desperately.

'Well, you can't – you just have to wait,' she replied. I hoped the crowded journey wouldn't last much longer, as to my horror, I noticed wet patches some children had left on their seats as they shuffled on them uncomfortably, trying to hide their predicament.

Chapter Five

'I'll take that one'

I almost fell out of my seat as the train screeched to a halt. Hetty and Mary were looking as confused as I felt. But where were we? Looking up, I saw a huge board with the name Icklesham painted on it. The name meant nothing to me. Suddenly there was pandemonium.

'Oi, you! Give me my shoes back, I'm getting off first!' said one of the boys who'd been sitting on the luggage rack, as he jumped to the floor. Hetty produced them from behind her back and handed them over.

Then turning to me, she said, 'Come on, Kitty, grab your pillowcase and gas mask. Looks like we're here,' as everyone began pushing and shoving to get off the train. We stepped onto the station platform.

The station was so small it reminded me of the pretend station that was Billy's favourite toy back home. My initial excitement began to give way to weariness and apprehension. I just wanted to go home. The hundreds of children I had seen on the platform in London all seemed to be on the platform here, milling about together, making the space unbearably crowded.

'Now, all form a queue so I can give you all some nourishment,' shouted Miss Giblin.

'It's not nourishment I need, it's a toilet,' I told Hetty. After we'd been counted, we were each offered an apple and either milk or water. Hating warm milk, I chose water which was also in a milk bottle. Then I joined the long queue for the only two toilets available. It seemed everyone needed the toilet. The long queue was made up mainly of girls. The boys appeared to have found another solution. I started to feel more comfortable but then began to panic – everything suddenly seemed chaotic. After leaving the dirty, smelly toilet, I couldn't find Hetty and was frantic. There were unfamiliar children everywhere. Feeling alone and frightened, I began to cry. A woman with the WVS green hat and a file tucked under her arm took my hand.

'What's wrong with you?' she asked.

'Can't find my big sister,' I sobbed.

'Don't worry, I'll take care of you – just stay with me,' she said as she wiped my eyes with a lace handkerchief. We walked around until we found Hetty and Mary. Hetty was angry and showed me no sympathy.

'It's your own fault. I can't have eyes in the back of my head – hold onto me,' she said as she grabbed my wrists roughly. Holding onto the string on her gas mask, I vowed to myself that I'd never let her go again.

Some teachers had travelled with us, but now there were special women in charge. Miss Giblin had disappeared and there were only strangers accompanying us. More WVS volunteers appeared and were talking to other women who seemed to be offering them advice, handing them papers and pointing to us. These women were also wearing labels, though all I could work out were the words 'billeting officer'. I later learnt that billeting officers were responsible for finding accommodation for evacuees. The billeting officers helped the WVS women to line us all up and then march us down a cobbled street. We passed a butcher's shop where a man was standing in the doorway dressed in a white coat and blue-and-white striped apron. He looked angry. As we walked up the hill with our pillowcases and gas masks, we passed a small grocery shop. In a corner stood a group of women who all turned to stare at us. Some of the children gave them a friendly wave, but they didn't wave back. We were all so weary now. It felt as though we'd been walking for miles, although it couldn't really have been very far. Eventually we arrived at what we thought was a house, but which we discovered was a school. Once inside, in the small school hall, we were all told to line up against a wall.

'Put your backs against the wall and stand up straight!' shouted a woman with a green hat. The excitement had now all faded and we were wondering what was going on. Some children were crying and wanted to go home. This couldn't have been further from the birthday surprise I was expecting.

'Boys over there and girls the other side!' the woman shouted. We were all confused and wondered why we were being sorted out like dirty washing. What, I wondered, was happening to the brothers and sisters who'd travelled together? 'Big boys this end,' she said. Why was that – what was she going to do to them? Alfie went to the other end of the hall with all the bigger boys, and I was now beginning to feel afraid again. Alfie, however, didn't seem to care. He was almost enjoying the experience. Pulling up his socks and running his hand across his face to move his tousled hair, he went off grinning.

In a corner, a nurse in a blue dress and white apron, with a white hat perched on her head, sat at a table on which there was a small white enamel bowl with a blue rim. Next to the bowl was a comb and I caught the familiar odour of antiseptic. I had my suspicions about this. We were told to file past the nurse. After a brief look at our arms and hands, she took each child in turn and roughly passed the comb through their hair, following this with a close inspection of the comb as she searched carefully for any infestation. A bit late, I thought. Mum did that every Friday: I hated it and would often disappear, hoping to avoid it, but now I felt grateful in the knowledge I would pass the test.

By now it was early evening and we were all increasingly tired, afraid and hungry. But I felt lucky: I had my big sisters with me and was sorry for the children who were kept to one side because the nurse had discovered nits. A disgusting-looking fluid with a horrible smell was combed through their hair.

Suddenly, we were awoken from our exhaustion as a crowd of grown-ups came through an open door. These people looked strange to me and most of them wore woollen hats and wellingtons. They walked past us very slowly. I wondered why they were there. Despite the fact that some smiled, they didn't look particularly friendly. They seemed to be scrutinising each of us from head to toe. I wished I had a suitcase instead of the pillowcase with the string running through the top. At least my hair was clean – some of the children looked so dirty after the long journey. I clung to my sisters as the sea of strange, unfriendly faces walked past us.

'I'll take that one,' one woman called, pointing to a girl in Hetty's class. *Take her where? Where on earth is she taking her? Where is she going?* These thoughts raced through my mind.

'Betty Holland, step forward. Off you go with the nice lady!' shouted the WVS volunteer. The woman who took Betty was thin and had a bright red shawl over her hunched shoulders. Betty looked terrified and I felt sorry for her. As she went off, she turned to look at Hetty with tears in her eyes. We never saw her again.

'What'll happen to her? Where's she going?' I asked Hetty and Mary, as Betty walked off meekly into the unknown. Hetty had tears in her eyes.

'I need to go to the toilet,' I said to Hetty.

'Not again – you can't,' she replied. Feeling exhausted, I slid down and sat on the floor.

'Stand up!' shouted the WVS woman.

'I want to go home,' I said. This didn't feel like much of a birthday.

'You can't. Shut up and stop moaning,' said Hetty. Why was Hetty so cross and what was she cross about? All I wanted to know was when we were going home. Each time an adult pointed to a child, a WVS woman would jot the child's name down on a piece of paper. Then, and this was what frightened me most of all, they were taken away by the stranger who'd pointed their finger at them. Thoughts rushed through my head. *What is it with these people? Who are they? They don't seem to like girls. Why aren't Mum and Dad with us?* Funnily enough, it seemed that all the boys had a finger pointed at them before most of the girls. For some reason, it was usually the big boys who were chosen. Alfie, in Mary's class, was the first to have the pointed finger treatment and he was as big as an ox! He went off with a cocky walk and a smile on his face because he'd been picked first, but I knew he was scared. He always walked that way when he was afraid. I'd noticed it sometimes just before a fight in the school playground.

'Bye, see you later,' he said as he swaggered off with his gas mask swinging round his neck and his pillowcase tucked under his arm. To distract myself from my fears, I began to concentrate on the hall we were all in. It was small and had a strange musty smell. Dark brown tiles reached halfway up the walls. Above these, the walls were painted white but were beginning to yellow. In a corner of the room, there was a cracked wooden door with a bolt and a latch to open it. A pile of chairs was stacked up in another corner. No one thought to use these. We were simply told to stand up straight.

This system of selecting children continued until it was quite late and getting dark outside. Once or twice a pointed finger was directed at Mary, but the woman in the green hat explained that Mary had two sisters and we had to stay together.

Stay together where? I wondered. Hetty explained to anyone who looked interested that she was in charge of the toothpaste and *that* was the reason we couldn't be separated. The strangers showed no interest in us and walked on to find someone without a toothpaste problem. I was beginning to feel pleased about having to share. Now and then Hetty would tidy my hair and straighten my dress, as if we were on show. All I wanted to do was sit on the floor, but I wasn't allowed to do so. By now my sisters and I were the only children in the hall. The number of grown-ups with the pointy fingers who came in to look at us was diminishing rapidly, and we were beginning to feel cold and hungry.

Suddenly, a woman came in with a boy at her side. He looked older than Hetty, about sixteen. It was a little strange to see a real country boy. He wore an oversized green jumper, black wellingtons and a black woollen hat on top of masses of red hair. He bent over and whispered to the woman, who might have been his mother. It seemed to me that the boy had noticed Mary's long, curly blonde hair and had decided to choose her. The woman pointed to Mary, uttering the now familiar words, 'I'll take that one.' I felt so afraid and clung to Hetty's arm. Could I be the next one to be taken into the unknown? Once again, Hetty protested, saying that our mum wouldn't allow us to be separated. She was very brave to do so and I was so grateful that she did, but the billeting officer was now holding the file with her pen poised, ready to cross Mary off.

'I'm afraid we'll have to split you up. No one is ever going to have the three of you.'

'No, I'm sorry, that's not possible – we're sisters,' said Hetty, but her objections fell on deaf ears. We clung onto Mary but to no avail. The billeting officer put her hand on Mary's shoulder and gently pushed her forward. Uncharacteristically, Mary was close to tears and made it clear that she didn't want to leave us, putting her arm through Hetty's and clinging on tightly. But it seemed her fate was sealed.

The woman who took Mary seemed kind, the sort of person you might pick if you had to have your sister taken away by someone, but I still didn't trust her. She patted me on the head, told me she would take good care of Mary and that we'd see her soon. She was smartly dressed compared with everyone else who'd walked through the door. She wore a brown skirt, beige stockings and brown shoes. She carried a walking stick but didn't have grey hair and looked younger than Mum. Despite the promise and the big smile, taking Mary off alone was going to split us up and that was something Mum had made us promise never to let happen. Mary had no toothpaste.

Sometimes when we ran out at home, we'd use salt – maybe the woman might give her some.

'Don't cry,' said Hetty. 'We'll find her tomorrow.'

'Of course you will,' said the billeting officer. Opening her large file, she crossed Mary's name off her list. Unable to argue with the woman in the green hat and the billeting officer any more, Hetty and I had to give in. Mary went away with her funny piggy mask in a cardboard box and her pillowcase with the string threaded through the top. These two items formed a cross on her back and to me the cross looked like a kiss goodbye. She looked very upset but seemed reassured by Hetty's promise that she would see her later. Little did I know it would be almost a year before we would see her again.

It was getting darker. Hetty and I wondered whether or not it was a good thing to be the last to be picked. Perhaps no one would choose us and they'd send us home on the next train? Then I could play with my new doll and we could come and collect Mary the next day.

After what seemed like an eternity, a young woman rushed in. She looked flustered and in a hurry. She was dressed in a brown coat and wellington boots, with a green scarf covering her head, and she was carrying a big straw bag. Although we didn't mind her appearance, we didn't like her attitude. She wasn't interested in us at all, and just seemed to want to get in and out as quickly as possible.

'Have you any left?' she asked the billeting officer.

'You can have those two,' came the reply as she pointed to Hetty and me.

'Oh, I only wanted one – but if that's all you have, I'll take them both off your hands.'

The billeting officer smiled broadly and gently pushed us forward. 'Isn't that kind of the lady?' she said to us.

By this time, we were glad to have been chosen. At least we would be together. I even tried to make myself believe that the woman might have been taking us out of kindness. We later discovered that these country folk had to have a really good reason *not* to take an evacuee, and that they were paid to take children into their homes.

Hetty and I were bundled into a car and driven off through the dark. Where was she taking us? The car was very dirty, with bits of straw everywhere. It also had a strong doggy smell. But we were grateful to be sitting down at last, and the smell was the least of our worries.

Chapter Six

Were we being kidnapped?

We had to endure yet another weary journey, winding through the countryside in the car. We began to wonder if we'd ever find Mary again, as we seemed to be driving further and further from the school where we'd been pointed at and picked up. The young woman who was driving didn't utter a word through the entire journey. Even when we asked her about Mary, she didn't reply and that made me sad and worried.

'Do you know where our sister went?' Hetty asked hopefully, her face strained and worried. Was something so terrible about to happen to Mary that she felt she couldn't tell us? Or was the young woman ignoring us because she didn't like us? What lay ahead of us? Everything seemed so unreal. Were we being kidnapped? We were so afraid. No houses, no buildings – just dark, winding roads. Finally, we reached a huge iron gate. Was this a prison? But it couldn't be, as the gates were wide open and we were driving through them onto a long gravel path. Bending down to peer through the front window, we saw what looked like a castle, just like those I'd seen in picture books. It was surrounded by gardens and trees, flowers and grass. Even in the dark, it looked like a park, but without the swings. It looked wonderful, fit for a princess. Hetty squeezed my hand and smiled. It would be big enough for Mary as well when we found her. We were driven up to the front of the great house, where the car took a sharp turn and made its way to the back. As we reached the back entrance, our driver finally spoke.

'Get out, you two, and take your rubbish down those steps and wait for me.' She spoke with a strange accent and was very abrupt. We fumbled our way in the dark, down an even darker staircase.

'Hang onto me. Give me your pillowcase – I'll hold that. Just go slowly,' said Hetty. The stairs were steep and made of soft, crumbly stone. It felt creepy and I clung onto Hetty even more tightly. She too clung onto me in case I fell. At the bottom was a narrow concrete corridor, at the end of which were two wooden doors. We waited some time for something to happen, too scared to shout and attract the woman's attention. We were very cold as well as tired. At last, the woman reappeared and pushed open one of the doors. A dim light hung from the ceiling and, to our dismay, on the floor we could see a big mattress with two folded grey blankets on top. We walked slowly over to the mattress, noticing that the blankets had red stitching all round them. They felt hard and itchy. There weren't even any pillows, so I made up my mind that I would stuff the pillowcase Mum had given me and use that beneath my head. Looking around, we saw a small table in the corner, a small stool and a mirror on the wall. The walls were bare brick, something I'd never seen before inside a home. We were in the basement and there were bars across the very small window that looked out into the night sky. The room felt like a prison. Though it was clean, it had a musty smell. It didn't look in the least comfortable.

'This is your room. Get to bed now and I'll call you in the morning,' the woman said.

I was determined I wasn't going to spoil my new pyjamas on *this* mattress. They were my pride and joy, so they remained neatly folded. Tiredness overcame us and as Hetty cuddled me, promising we'd run away and find Mary the next day, we fell asleep on the blanket, still dressed in our clothes. Suddenly, after what seemed like just a few minutes, the young woman who'd driven us there opened the door.

'Time to get up!' she shouted. 'Get up, you two.' We thought it was the middle of the night as it was still dark, but it was early in the morning. We scrambled off the blanket. A gentle breeze was coming through the little barred window. We walked down a small passage and through a door that led into a vast kitchen. It was warm and I could smell food. We were hungry, not having had anything to eat since leaving London.

'That's for you,' the woman said, pointing to a large bowl of bread and hot milk. She wasn't looking at us, and she seemed flushed, her cheeks bright red. Her hair was tied back, forming a tiny bun shape. We sat on high stools at a great big table and tucked into the bowl in front of us. Bread and milk wasn't normally my favourite food, but that morning it tasted delicious.

Hetty smiled at her and said, 'Thank you very much. That was so nice.' Hetty thought we might be offered more, but the woman didn't reply. Awed, I looked around the kitchen. There were so many different things everywhere – huge trays, cutlery, teapots and sugar bowls. Shiny pots and pans were hanging on the walls. In a glass cupboard there were stacks of china. I was amazed by the size of the sink and the cooking stove, which had eight rings.

'Hurry up!' the woman said. 'My name is Rosie, but you will call me Miss Rosie. I work very hard here for the lord and lady of the house and I don't have time to look after you. I didn't want you here in the first place, so you'll have to help me here in the kitchen if we're to get along.'

'Well, we didn't want to be here either,' said Hetty. It seemed a row was brewing, but Miss Rosie stood firm with her arms folded and seemed to ignore Hetty's risky comment.

'Now go and wash your hands and face over there,' she said, pointing to the large sink. 'The toilet is just outside your bedroom, out in the courtyard. Once you're finished, get back here quickly.'

On one wall hung a bell and next to it was a spotless apron. Miss Rosie, whom we discovered was the maid, always wore a grubby apron. When the bell rang, she'd rush to swap her dirty apron for the clean one. Once back in the kitchen, she'd change her clean apron back to the grubby one. Where did she go? I was later to find out that she was responding to the call of the lady of the house, and would wear a clean apron while she attended her. I wondered about this mystery lady. Who was she? Did she even know we were here? It would seem not. It was left entirely to Miss Rosie to take care of us. And where were we? I later discovered that we were in a manor house in Sussex.

Miss Rosie didn't seem much older than Hetty. She had a lovely head of curls and chubby red cheeks. Was that why she was called Rosie? A short, round, plump girl, she always wore a black skirt and jumper, black woollen stockings and flat black shoes with, of course, the grubby apron on top of it all. It turned out that Rosie was both the maid and the cook.

The toilet was just a bucket with a plank of wood across it, and it smelt so awful it made my eyes water. Cracks in the door, which had no bolt, meant that when using the toilet, I had to stretch my leg out to keep the door closed. With big spiders tucked away in the corners, you would try to get out of there as quickly as possible. At home, the toilet was the place where we would comfortably read our comics.

Wondering why it was so dark outside, I noticed a large clock on my way back to the house. It was five o'clock in the morning! Once we'd cleaned ourselves, we returned to the kitchen. In the centre of the room, the huge table where we'd had our bread and milk was now covered with all sorts of silverware. Again, I was struck by all the paraphernalia in front of me: teapots, silver of all shapes and sizes, and even toast racks. I didn't even know toast had its own racks.

There were also large silver trays which were very heavy to lift.

'You two must clean the silver as part of your keep here – but be quick, as you won't want to be late for school on your first day,' said Rosie. I was used to doing chores at home, but this job looked as if it would take for ever. We rubbed and shone with the rags Rosie had given us.

'Just let us do what we can or we'll never get out of here,' Hetty said after some time. She was being so brave. It was now eight o'clock and we were told to wash our hands and get ready for school. For the first time in my life, the word 'school' sounded like music to my ears. It made the task we were doing almost bearable. With the thought of going to school and perhaps seeing Mary there, we rubbed the silver even more vigorously.

Our street party for the coronation of George VI in 1937. My grandparents, my parents and Billy in the pram, are in the bottom right hand corner. I'm sitting at the table next to the couple dressed in Union Jack suits

Me, Mum and Billy in mourning after Charlie died

Me, Hetty, Billy and Mary at Moffat House, Camberwell

Mum and Nan

The last telegram we received from Dad, sent while he was in Italy in 1944

Dad in his army uniform in Italy in 1944

Me aged thirteen

Cas/167/1951

Infantry Record Office,
Stanwell Road School,
ASHFORD, Middlesex.

Mrs. H. Baxter,
5, Moffat House,
Comber Grove,
LONDON S.E.6.

17th April, 1944.

Madam,

      Information has now come to hand of a change in the date on which your husband, No. 6208434, Private William BAXTER, The Middlesex Regiment, was reported to have died of wounds.

      It now transpires that the correct date was 5th April, 1944 and not 6th April, 1944, as previously reported.

      An amended notification is enclosed and it would be appreciated if you would return the notification on which the incorrect date was stated, which was forwarded to you on 13th April, 1944.

      An envelope is enclosed for the purpose and I would like, if I may, to add my personal condolences to the sympathy and regret expressed by the Army Council.

                I am, Madam,
                Your obedient servant,

                Major for Colonel,
                i/c Infantry Records, ASHFORD, Middlesex.

WBC.

Enclosures 2/

The second letter we received in 1944 from Infantry Record Office telling us that Dad had died

Dad's grave at Monte Cassino in Italy

Me revisiting Moffat House in Camberwell

Chapter Seven

Searching for Mary

We believed we'd only have to go to school for a short time – because as soon as we found Mary, we'd make our own way back to London to Mum and Dad and our brothers.

'It won't be long now until we find Mary, and we'll walk if we have to,' said Hetty as she clutched my hand tightly and straightened my dress, which was now looking very crumpled and grubby.

We had to go to school in the same clothes we'd travelled in, and Miss Rosie drew a little map for us on the back of an envelope. As we tried to follow her instructions, we found ourselves on paths that took us into fields. It felt strange to be outside with no buildings around, and I could almost have enjoyed it if everything hadn't seemed so confusing. We passed leafy hedges and a little stream which I longed to put my feet into.

It also felt strange and a little frightening not seeing anyone else on our way. Back in Camberwell, we were used to shops, trams, lots of people and children playing everywhere. If only Mum was around to help us find Mary. We had no idea where we were going but we continued walking, trying to follow Rosie's map.

'Come on. We can't stop. Let's get to this school and find Mary,' Hetty said.

The countryside was full of many different shades of colour and had none of the nasty smells of London. I knew berries grew on bushes, but Hetty explained to me that milk came from cows. I wasn't that keen on that, and decided to drink water in the future. We even saw apples growing on trees, but Hetty told me that they'd be poisonous and we shouldn't touch them. Only apples bought in shops could be eaten, she said. Despite the wonder of it all, I suddenly, desperately wanted to be back home. In one field, we came face to face with what we thought was a huge cow. Or was it a bull? Its big brown eyes stared at us and its long tail swished from side to side; did that mean it was angry? We'd never seen cattle so close before – only in the distance when we went hop-picking. Whatever it was, it looked bad-tempered and we decided to take the long way round the field. We thought we could explain to the teacher why we were late and, as it was our first day, we were convinced she'd understand.

Eventually, we arrived at a small brick building. It looked like a house, and was surrounded by a low wooden fence. When we first saw it, Hetty said it couldn't possibly be a school and that we must have taken a wrong turning when we tried to avoid the animals in the field. It looked so small and nothing like the big school back home in Camberwell. Pushing open a little wooden gate, we walked down a gravel path to a green wooden door with a latch. We slowly walked in and saw a group of children sitting in pairs at tiny desks. A smell of polish hung in the air. The white paint on the walls was flaking off. Every desk had a little hole in it containing ink. The children looked as though their ages ranged from about five to fourteen. The younger children were sitting in the first few rows and the bigger ones behind. They weren't wearing uniforms, as we did in London, and their clothes made the classroom look so full of colour that for a split second, I felt I could almost like this place. Some of the children were even wearing woollen hats. As we walked into the classroom, a gasp came from them and every head turned towards us. I wanted to run out but it was too late.

'Can we leave here? I don't like this silly school – it's not a real school,' I said to Hetty.

'Who are you?' asked the teacher. She was tall and thin with glasses on the end of her nose. 'What do you think you are doing, walking in here? Where did you come from?' She sat at a desk with small steps on each side.

'We're from London,' Hetty said proudly. The children burst into giggles and I grabbed hold of Hetty's skirt, as I was beginning to feel a little afraid.

'We seem to have lost our way today,' I explained, feeling myself shaking. 'It's our first day. We're very sorry.'

'Well, we can't have that.' the teacher said. 'We abide by the rules here. Come over here to me.' We both walked meekly through all the rows of desks to the front of the class.

'Hold out your hand,' the teacher instructed me. Was she going to give me a sweet, as she felt sorry for me? How wrong I was.

'Hold out your arm, you stupid child, palm up,' she said. Why were all the children laughing behind their hands? What was she going to do? Suddenly, from behind her desk she withdrew what looked like a stick. Before I realised what was happening, she'd whacked me three times across my fingers. Tears welled in my eyes and I looked at Hetty in shock. I thought Hetty was going to whack the teacher – she looked so angry. She gave me a hug and under her breath she whispered, 'Don't cry. Pretend you don't care.' Then it was Hetty's turn.

After we'd been punished, the teacher looked at us with eyes that seemed to lack any emotion. 'Don't be late again. We don't have any spare chairs, so go and sit on the floor at the back of the class,' she said sternly.

We walked, heads held high, between the grinning children and sat cross-legged at the back of the class as we were told. We sat there for the rest of the day, not daring to speak. I looked around and wondered why we were the only two from London. Where were all the hundreds of children we'd seen at the station? We were alone with no friends. And where was Mary?

There was only one classroom in the whole school. No one spoke to us all day and we dared not speak, not even to each other. Once or twice, when I knew the answer to an English or sums question, my hand went up, but I was completely ignored and so eventually we gave up bothering. In any case, the work seemed so much easier than the work we'd been doing in our London school. We found everything about the school backward and boring. At three o'clock, the teacher rang a large hand bell. It was time to go back to Miss Rosie, but we still hadn't found Mary. Perhaps she too had lost her way and we'd see her the next day.

We were out at last in the courtyard. Some of the children made a circle round us, which made us nervous. We also noticed that other children were keeping their distance. One of the boys, a largish lad who was wearing what looked like an apron to keep his clothes clean, was being egged on by the other children.

'Go on, Simon, out, out!' they chanted. I grabbed onto Hetty.

'Don't do anything, Hetty,' I pleaded. She was very angry and put her arm round me. Simon walked past us holding his nose. Hetty grabbed his hat from his head and threw it over the fence.

The teacher came running out into the courtyard. She hadn't seen Simon holding his nose, only Hetty grabbing the hat. 'Don't bring your bad London habits to our school. I will not tolerate it!' she said, as she pulled on Hetty's jumper and dragged her back into the classroom.

'Leave her alone!' I shouted. 'He started it.' Poor Hetty took another caning. This didn't stop Simon holding his nose every day thereafter, whenever he passed us. To get our own back, we'd poke out our tongues, with our thumbs on our noses and fingers outstretched, making certain the teacher didn't see us. Most of the children would behave like this towards us. It didn't bother us much though, as our minds were firmly set on finding Mary and then going back to London.

We started to find our own way back to Miss Rosie at the manor house. By planning a different route each day, we thought we might find Mary. We were in no hurry to get back and enjoyed the country walk. We kept calling out 'Mary! Mary!' in the hope that she might hear us, but all we heard was our own echo. We'd only known noisy city streets before.

Once we were back in our billet, as it became known, it was nearly five o'clock. When Miss Rosie saw us she said, 'Oh, it's you two.'

Miss Rosie hadn't asked us our names and never did. It was always 'you two'. She told us to wash our hands and sit down in the kitchen. In front of us was placed a bowl of delicious-looking vegetable soup with a plate of home-made bread. As it was the first thing we'd eaten since the bread and milk that morning, it was very welcome and tasted good.

'Oh, thank you, that was so good. Is there any more?' Hetty dared to ask. Miss Rosie gave us a beaming smile and refilled our bowls. At last we felt full. She never let us go hungry. The country air gave me a good appetite. In London, I was always the last to finish my plate and would never have eaten all the vegetables in that soup.

'Now, wash your hands and go to bed,' said Miss Rosie.

We couldn't believe that we were being asked to go to bed so early. At home, we never went to bed before nine o'clock, and it was only six o'clock now. But we didn't say a word. It had been a long day and we'd been up so early. At least we didn't have more cleaning to do, and we thought if we argued with Miss Rosie, she might give us another job.

Back in our room, we found a boxed game of Ludo on the mattress and played while we chatted, planning to take longer to get back from school in future so that the evenings would seem shorter. Later in our stay, Miss Rosie also produced a game of Snakes and Ladders, but we still preferred to take our time coming back to our billet. We took a long time trying to fulfil our mission of finding Mary by knocking on cottage doors and asking if anyone had seen her.

I eventually realised that we were probably in the servants' quarters, but wondered where the other servants were. Was Miss Rosie the only servant in this great house, apart from the old man in the garden, who sometimes joined us for soup in the evening? He was always kind to us, patting us on the head as he walked by, and was our only source of warmth and comfort in that situation. He had bright red cheeks and long white whiskers down each side of his face. We discovered that he was the gardener who grew all the vegetables for the soup we enjoyed so much. Whenever we saw him, he would always touch his cap and give us a big smile and a wink. Although he never spoke to us, his smile and cheery manner made us feel we had a friend. I sometimes saw him in the garden with a beautiful black dog, but he never brought the dog into the kitchen.

The first weeks passed slowly. None of the children at the school mixed with us and the teacher had no intention of teaching us. We remained at the back of the class and were finally given individual chairs but no desk. No one thought to give us a pencil or paper, so we just tried to listen – but the teacher spoke in a way that was strange to us and we found it hard to understand her. One day we took our Snakes and Ladders game to school, but it was taken away from us and we never got it back.

Every Friday, Miss Rosie would put a tin bath in our room. We filled this with warm water, heated using saucepans from the kitchen. Miss Rosie said the rule was not to use more than five inches of water, so it didn't take us long to get the bath ready. We would also wash our clothes in the bathwater and dry them in the yard outside.

At some point during these early days, it began to dawn on me that we hadn't been kidnapped, but I still didn't understand what was happening. Why had we been sent away to a place we didn't know and to people we had never met? And above all, where was Mary?

Unbeknown to me, on the day that I had left London for what I thought was my birthday surprise, children all over England were also leaving their homes and travelling to different, safer parts of the country. War was about to be declared and the children were being moved away from danger, especially the threat of bombs landing on or near their homes. Many children were evacuated on ships and sent abroad. There was opposition within the government, but despite this, the scheme went ahead.

One tragedy occurred when a German submarine fired a torpedo on the SS *City of Benares*, a passenger ship that was bound for Canada with 100 evacuees on board. The ship sank almost at once. Many children drowned immediately, but some were put into lifeboats and left to the mercy of the sea. Two days later, a rowing boat was spotted with twenty young boys on board, aged between five and twelve. At first sight, it was thought that these children were survivors of the attack and were asleep from exhaustion. But further inspection revealed that they'd all died from exposure. Twelve days later, another lifeboat was found but fortunately all the children on board were alive. Over seventy children lost their lives on the SS *City of Benares*.

Many years later, I met one of the survivors of this tragedy, by then a man in his seventies. He told me that aged eleven, he'd been on the ship in charge of his younger brother aged seven, who'd been unwell and in the sickbay when the torpedo struck. On the impact of the blast, someone had grabbed the younger brother and pulled him onto a lifeboat. The two brothers had been separated, each on a different lifeboat. It later transpired that this man's younger brother was one of the boys picked up on the lifeboat on which all the children had died. He'd been recognised by the name on his jacket. The man told me how, since that dreadful day, he'd never been able to get close to anyone, not even his own son, for fear they might suddenly be taken away from him. He also confessed that he'd never recovered from the guilt he felt in losing the brother he was supposed to have been taking care of.

There was another tragedy of the war that would also touch my own life a long time later. At a certain point in the war, Germans and Italians living in Britain, known as 'enemy aliens', were considered a threat. A famous phrase of the then prime minister, Winston Churchill, was 'Collar the lot', which meant that any Italians and Germans living in England had to be rounded up for fear that they were or might become spies. They had to be deported whether or not they posed a risk to Britain. Churchill was taking no chances. A ship called the SS *Arandora Star*, once a cruise ship, was commandeered by the British government to take these so-called enemy aliens to Canada. The ship was painted grey and sailed without the safety of the Red Cross, which would have protected it. The German submarine that sunk it believed it to be a warship. The SS *Arandora Star* was carrying 1,500 people when it was torpedoed. Eight hundred passengers, both German and Italian, as well as British crew members, lost their lives. Many bodies were washed up on the Irish coast and buried as 'unknown' in Ireland.

Many years later, I discovered that one of the passengers who died was my children's grandfather, the father of my Italian husband, who was just a child at the time. Like many others, his father had come to London as a young man to work, had married, had two sons and built up a small business. He'd lived in London for almost twenty years, but had never taken British nationality and still had an Italian passport. All he had wanted was to improve his life and that of his future family.

Chapter Eight

The reunion

Many months had passed since our arrival in the countryside. Every night we sat in our billet planning to run away, wondering how we could get a train without money. 'We'll just pay the other end,' said Hetty as she sat drawing a little map. We tirelessly continued to wander around searching for Mary both during the week and at weekends, but our efforts were in vain. We didn't want to run away before we'd found her. As we wandered round the countryside searching for her, we picked wild flowers to put in our room. In a ditch, we found a small empty tin can which we used as a vase. This was something we couldn't do in London. There were so many flowers to choose from in the woods and beside the stream. 'Don't pick the long grasses – they won't fit in the can,' Hetty advised as she lay back staring up at the sky.

We missed Mum, Dad, Billy and Charlie so much, and while enjoying the countryside we also longed for pie and mash from our local shop. and the fish and chips that Dad sometimes treated us to. If we didn't have any money for fish, we'd be given a bag of crackling or even just a bag of chips.

Every day we looked out for a letter from Mum, but none ever came. We didn't understand why and thought she might have forgotten us. Or perhaps she didn't know where we were.

After what seemed like years, but was in fact just eight months, we arrived back at our billet one Saturday afternoon after a busy time still searching for Mary. To our absolute joy, we saw Mum sitting in the kitchen alongside Miss Rosie, sipping a mug of tea and chatting to her like an old friend.

As we walked into the kitchen, Mum jumped up with arms outstretched. We were overcome with emotion and shock, as we'd started to believe that we'd never see her again. In no time, our pillowcases were packed and by Mum's side, my new pyjamas still folded and unused. After tears and hugs, we clung to Mum and, keeping my arms round her neck, I wouldn't let her go. Then came the magic words: 'I'm taking you home.' It was unbelievable. All our dreams had come true.

'But we can't, Mum, we haven't found Mary yet,' Hetty said. 'We've searched everywhere.'

'She's meeting us at the station,' Mum replied. How could Mum have managed to get in touch with her? I looked up at Miss Rosie, expecting her to confirm that we'd been searching for Mary since our arrival. Miss Rosie turned her face away, but her cheeks were reddening.

'Come on, let's get a move on, else you'll miss that London train,' Miss Rosie said as she picked up my packed pillowcase.

She looked worried. As we were leaving, Miss Rosie handed a bundle of paper to Hetty, saying, 'A little present for you.'

They were letters, all opened, to us from Mum. It transpired that Mum had indeed written to us, but

Miss Rosie had opened all the letters without passing them on to Hetty and me. The letters had told us where to find Mary, so while we'd spent months searching, Miss Rosie had known Mary's whereabouts all along.

We stood there, unable to take in the fact of what she'd done. Miss Rosie then went on to explain to Mum, uncomfortably, that looking for Mary had given us something to do. She also said that she hadn't given us the letters because she didn't want to upset us with thoughts of home. If only she'd known how upset we'd been *not* knowing where to find Mary, and *not* hearing from Mum.

We had hardly anyone to say goodbye to, as during our stay with Miss Rosie we'd never met the lord and lady of the manor house. Although the manor house resembled a castle, we'd been confined to the kitchen, courtyard and downstairs bedroom. Our goodbyes were swift. As we were leaving, we were lucky enough to find our garden friend, whom we used to call Grandad, and we said our goodbyes to him. He shook Mum's hand and handed her a small parcel in a tiny sack, tied at the top with string.

'This is for you,' he said in his strong country accent. I implored Mum to let us come back one day to see him, the only person who'd shown us real kindness.

Mum took the parcel with a smile. She looked so smart and I was so proud of her. She shook his hand and thanked him for his kindness to us. He put his finger to his lips, indicating that she shouldn't speak, as Miss Rosie might disapprove of his giving her a gift. It was now early evening and this lovely moment was suddenly interrupted by Miss Rosie tooting the horn on her car.

'Hurry up, or you'll miss the train. There ain't another one today,' Rosie called out. We were soon back inside the smelly, dirty car that she'd collected us in so many months before.

Mary was there at the station with Dad. I flung my arms round Dad – it was wonderful to see him. Mary looked so grown-up, wearing a pale blue coat with dark blue velvet collar, black patent ankle strap shoes, white ankle socks edged with lace and a small matching bag across her shoulder. She looked like a princess, but I sensed a sadness about her. We were overjoyed to see her, but she wouldn't even look at us and seemed a little distant, hiding behind Dad. 'Don't she know me?' I asked Mum. Mum put her arm round me, telling me to be patient. Perhaps after such a long time Mary was shy at seeing us again. But even my huge smile wasn't returned. She turned her head away.

'Don't worry about her – she's just being stuck up,' said Hetty.

We later found out that Mary had been very happy in her billet and hadn't in fact been many miles from us, although we'd never have found her. If we had, she probably wouldn't have come with us or even spoken to us. She'd found a new life and loved it. Unlike our school experience, she'd had private tuition. In fact, she didn't want to leave her new home and go back to London. This made Mum a little upset. Mary had found a great friend in the son of the house, whom she referred to as a brother. She'd had her own bedroom, which she knew she wouldn't have at home. Mum told her she could go back for a visit, as the people who'd looked after her had been so kind. Mary cried all the way home, missing her new family. She was no longer the worried, vulnerable little girl who'd left home several months earlier.

After fiddling for some time with the knot on the sack that the gardener had given her, Mum finally managed to open it. A smile lit up her face. Inside the sack were carrots, onions, potatoes and two big red tomatoes. She gently caressed the contents one by one and sat with her parcel on her lap all the way home, treating it like gold, saying she hadn't seen some of those vegetables for quite some time. As the noisy old train started its long journey, I snuggled up to Mum who put her comforting arm round me. I'd already put that awful school and bedroom behind me and vowed never to leave home again. Little did I know what was ahead.

Chapter Nine

The phoney war and the real war

It was ten o'clock by the time we arrived back in London that night. There was a breeze and it had started to rain, but it was wonderful to be back in the busy streets and then in our small flat. Mum had made us Spam fritters and mashed potato. We didn't usually like Spam but that day it tasted great and we tucked in without any grumbles. Billy was very shy but happy to have us all back together again. He seemed to have grown so much in that short time, and wouldn't allow me to pick him up for a kiss.

'Go away, I don't like kisses. I'm not a baby,' he said, running away to hide behind the kitchen door. Poor Mary was still crying: she'd got used to having her own bedroom and really wanted to go back to the country.

During our absence, Mum had made us a new eiderdown patterned with pink roses to match the curtains. 'Look how pretty our bedroom is,' said Hetty, trying to console Mary, but she continued to cry, saying she missed her brother. We reminded her that she had two brothers here at home in London, but she wasn't interested.

'What's that noise, Mum?' I asked as I got ready for bed, hearing footsteps, laughter and music from the surrounding flats.

'Well, it's good news. Mrs Edmunds from upstairs brought your friends, Jimmy, Freddy and Ruby home last week,' said Mum. After the silence of the country, I'd forgotten how noisy London was and wondered how I could bring the peace and colour of the countryside here to Camberwell. Camberwell Green was just up the road but there wasn't much green there. Nevertheless, it was so good to be back home and I couldn't wait to see all my friends upstairs again. The little doll I'd left on the windowsill was still there, her yellow painted head peeking out from the top of the brown paper bag, and still with the lace handkerchief wrapped around her.

We jumped into our cosy shared bed and no one complained about who pulled the most covers over or off them. We snuggled down to sleep, warm and happy. Our family was together again. We didn't know then that it would be for such a short time.

It wasn't long before Hetty and Mary started arguing again.

'Don't touch any of my clothes!' Mary shouted the next morning.

'Don't like them and anyway, they wouldn't fit me,' Hetty retorted. The new clothes Mary had brought back with her were very pretty. Looking at them, I wondered how long it would be before they'd be too small for her and could be passed on to me.

'Toast is ready!' Mum called out. The smell of the toast would bring us all together in our tiny warm kitchen. Great chunks of bread were spread out on our table and we had a choice of beef dripping or margarine spread. I loved the brown jelly that settled at the bottom of the dripping. Despite our arguing, it felt good to be together.

Although most children had been sent away suddenly on 1st September 1939 for fear of the German bombers attacking London, no bombing had in fact taken place. This period was known as the Phoney War. Now, believing London was safe, many hundreds of children like us had returned to their London families. Although some children had been badly treated by the people they were billeted with, many, like Mary, had been happy with their stay in the country and had been treated well – and many had remained with their foster parents. Some children even returned to their family in the countryside after the war, and remained there for many years.

Most of our friends had returned to London and it was so good to see them all. I didn't recognise my best friend Joan, who hadn't been evacuated. She seemed so grown-up. She'd lost her ponytail and had her hair in a very fashionable style.

'Hello, Kitty. Are you coming out?' she said shyly, as she walked into our kitchen.

Joan and I went everywhere together arm in arm, and her mum often allowed me to stay overnight in her flat. She always made me welcome even though my family couldn't return her kindness, as we simply didn't have the space. We no longer pushed around doll's prams: it was now clothes and boys that we giggled about most of the day. Most of the boys were still only interested in playing football in the courtyard, no matter how hard we tried to distract them.

Joan confessed to me how much she liked Big Billy. That was fine, because I fancied Alfie – but I knew Big Billy liked Daisy Jennings, who lived in another block of flats up the road, as I'd seen the two of them laughing and holding hands. However, not wanting to upset Joan, I kept that to myself. Big Billy had a little job in the shop, sorting, marking and delivering newspapers. He always had spending money in his pocket and he was a real grafter.

One thing at home was different. Looking through the back window, I could see a long, raised tunnel shape, stretching the whole length of the block of flats. This used to be an area of gravel and muddy grass. When I asked Mum what the shape was, she tried to reassure me. 'Don't worry about that, it's a lot of fuss for nothing. It's been so quiet here in London, I don't know why you all had to go away. Never mind, it's the past now. Thank goodness you're all home.' The shape was in fact an underground air raid shelter that had been dug out for the tenants of all the flats, and covered with grass, and big enough for about 100 people. It had a narrow entrance and while most of it was underground, there was a long, slightly raised bump just above ground level. We were to spend many terrifying nights in that shelter.

London had changed; people had changed. Many women were in uniform and everyone everywhere looked anxious. In the sky, there were huge balloons, looking like elephants with big ears. These were barrage balloons to defend us against aircraft attack.

It was September 1940 and I'd just had my tenth birthday. This brought the responsibility of keeping an eye on Billy. School hadn't yet returned to normal after the confusion of the evacuation. Most of the children were happy about this, not understanding how this lack of education could affect us in later life.

'Take Billy to the park, Kitty. At least it'll keep him away from the roads,' said Mum.

'Oh no, he's such a handful. I can't have any fun with him around,' I protested.

'Go on. Be a good girl. I'll make it up to you,' said Mum.

'But he runs off everywhere and I have to spend all my time trying to find him. Can't we go to the pictures? There's a good film on at the Regal this week and it's the last day,' I begged. Reluctantly, Mum gave us three pennies each.

'Try and get him in for nothing, as he's so little.' It was a nice sunny day and I longed to go to the park and meet up with friends, but I knew it would be easier to look after Billy in the cinema. I had it in mind to bunk in the side door. Maybe with the money Mum had given me, I could get us ice creams instead. As we ran off, Mum shouted, 'Hold his hand crossing the road!'

Just a few minutes up the road, we suddenly heard a weird noise coming from the sky. Looking up, I thought I saw masses of blackbirds. 'Take cover! Take cover!' everyone was shouting. What was going on and why was everyone running in all directions? The sun was in my eyes and I couldn't see clearly what was in the sky, but I grabbed Billy's hand and we ran back home as fast as we could. Mum was frantically running up the road towards us with Charlie in her arms. She seized Billy by his jumper and we all ran back towards our block of flats. The noise was caused by swarms of German bombers.

Once home, we all ran round the back of the flats to the big air raid shelter. It was horrible in that shelter, with the smell, the cold and the terrible noise from above. Most of our neighbours were already there, but Hetty and Mary had gone to the market in East Lane. Poor Mum was so worried but could do nothing. From the sound of the bombing, we thought no one would survive outside the shelter. Terrified, we just sat holding onto one another. After what seemed like for ever, but was actually a couple of hours, a long wailing noise told us it was now safe to emerge. This, we learnt, was the 'all clear', a noise we'd become all too familiar with. As we climbed up the stairs from the shelter, we saw rubble everywhere: houses were razed to the ground and you could taste the dust in the air.

Back in our flat, we tried to clear the mess of the shattered glass from many broken windows. Hetty and Mary suddenly appeared, white-faced and looking scared. They'd taken shelter nearby in a friend's house.

'Mrs Richardson made us go into her shelter in her garden,' Hetty said. Mum decided to prepare blankets and pillows to take down to the big shelter, should this ever happen again. After only a few hours, the dreadful siren was screeching once more. We each picked up a blanket and some warm clothing and ran back down to the shelter, where we were to remain all night.

This routine was to continue for at least eleven weeks. Both night and day, we'd run down to the shelter. Mum would grab Charlie and all his paraphernalia, while Hetty grabbed Billy. Along with Mary, I was in charge of all the blankets and drinking water.

'Hurry up, keep close to the wall and keep your head down,' Hetty would shout as we all ran to our smelly shelter, pulling whatever we could over our heads to shut out the noise of guns, planes and bombs.

Inside the shelter, there were about fifty metal bunk beds in blocks of three, mainly for the children and older neighbours. Mrs Rumble must have lived down there, as by the time we got there, she always had the best position and was sitting in her chosen place, surrounded by blankets and sandwiches, doing her knitting. 'Come on, luv, I've saved a place for you here,' she'd say. This would be the two bunk beds above her, which us children all shared, while Mum sat up all night. Click, click – Mrs Rumble's noisy knitting needles seemed to be clattering all night. Beside her sat a large bag full of balls of wool, all different colours.

'What do you think of this colour – will it go with this?' she'd ask, holding her knitting high for our approval.

'Yes, yes, that looks great,' we'd reply, trying to get some sleep.

This bombing started quite soon after we'd returned home from the country. The Phoney War was over. The Blitz had begun. Dad had joined the army and was only able to get home some weekends, so everything was left to Mum who was alone with five children. We missed him so much, but Mum was amazing, keeping us all together. Dad had joined the army following the news that Mum's brother had had such a bad time at Dunkirk, a front-line battle where many soldiers had died or been taken prisoner. Uncle Charlie had made it back home for a while, before being sent off to the front line again. Dad had volunteered to 'do his bit', as he said. He wouldn't normally have been asked to join the army, as he was older than the upper age limit for men.

Bombs were beginning to fall night and day and it was very hard for Mum to get us to the shelter in time. All the street lights and shop window lights were turned off, leaving us in darkness everywhere. We had to cover our windows with blackout curtains or blankets. Not a single chink of light was allowed to shine out. Mum sewed up all the holes in our curtains and used an old thick blanket to cover the windows. All windows had to have tape criss-crossed on them to prevent glass shattering over everything if they broke. Car headlights had to be covered and even a torch had to have a shield over the front of it, so as not to be seen by enemy bombers.

We began to go through some very frightening times. One attack on London lasted seventy-six consecutive nights. Sometimes it felt as if the world was coming to an end. But despite all this, I felt better being at home with Mum and the family, thinking that if we were going to be killed, at least we would all die together. The idea of being in the countryside and out of danger, but alone without my family, was out of the question. Our brave RAF pilots in their Spitfires kept many of the German Luftwaffe planes away. A young airman who lived in our block of flats sometimes came home on leave and I was madly in love with him. Sadly, he was killed on a night raid. I was heartbroken.

During these raids, we spent many hours in our shelter. At one end of the shelter there was a bucket covered by a wooden plank with a hole in it, hidden behind a curtain. This was it. The noise and smell that came from that toilet was disgusting and most people would take the risk of going outside to relieve themselves. 'Have you all been to the toilet?' Mum would ask, before we left the flat.

Many people were killed in road accidents because of the darkness in London. There were special wardens walking the streets, both men and women, who had to make certain no light could be seen anywhere. They were called air raid wardens, a service created to protect civilians. The air raid wardens were volunteers who, for various reasons, were unable to join the forces or were exempt such as doctors, police and some teachers. The familiar call of 'Put that light out!' became famous. There were also threats of a gas attack. The wardens were very strict and ensured that everyone carried their gas masks at all times.

The Home Guard kept watch on our coastlines and many other vital installations, like munitions factories. They were indispensable, as were rescue workers, ambulance drivers and people doing other similar essential jobs after air raids – such as digging up bodies or, even worse, parts of bodies.

Women had become vital to the war effort and most were happy to help. In fact, they often felt glad that they were able at last to earn their own money, doing jobs like making parts for the planes, ships and guns in factories that at one time had made sewing machines or even cars. The women who made munitions worked long and hard. It was dangerous work, as they were working with lethal chemicals which would turn their skin a yellow colour. For this reason, they were often referred to as the canary girls. They had no choice, as they were conscripted to either do war work or join the forces.

Many women were doing a wonderful job in the forces – the army, air force, navy or land army. These were mainly single women and they became very independent both socially and financially. They liked being in a position to earn their own money and although clothes were rationed with special coupons, they still managed to look glamorous. After the war, it was difficult for some women to give up their freedom: for women, like men, life was never going to be the same again.

Some people who lived in houses had their own private dugouts called Anderson shelters. They were made from corrugated iron and were buried deep in their own back gardens. These shelters were very small, built for one family. People sometimes covered them in earth and grew vegetables on top of them. Other people had Morrison shelters that remained inside the home. However, it really didn't matter which shelter you had as you were either lucky or not to survive each raid.

The dreaded sound of the siren, known as the Moaning Minnie, never seemed to cease. We each had to have a bag prepared with a drink, a bread roll, a book and a woollen jumper to sleep in. Mum wouldn't let me wear my new pyjamas as it was far too cold and damp in the shelter. We slept in our thick jumpers and stockings every night. Everyone tried to get the best place for the night, away from the smelly toilet and busy entrance. We'd all sing to drown out the noise of gunfire and falling bombs. Life was like a lottery and we lived one day at a time. We were exhausted through lack of sleep, but we had to cope and we did.

September 1940 brought with it the start of incendiary bombing. Firebombs lit up the sky over London. One night, a raid went on constantly from five in the evening until five the following morning, and on the night of 7th September 1940, 460 Londoners were killed. That number would rise to over 5,000 by the end of September. When we came up from the shelter after that night, once the 'all clear' had sounded, the sight before us was unbelievable. Buildings were had been flattened with many people still trapped beneath them. We were lucky that night as our block of flats was still standing and still is in 2022. Although we had no water or electricity for almost a week, Mum somehow managed. We were still alive.

Many much-loved dogs, cats and other domestic pets had to be put to sleep. The noise of bombs and gunfire was unbearable for them, so it was considered the kindest thing to do. The queue at the vets was long and it was sad to see all these unhappy people trying to do the best for their beloved pets.

If there were no air raids during the day, Billy and all the other children would play on the bomb sites – but it had to be within Mum's sight so she could get us quickly down the shelter, which was now accessible through a wooden gate or by climbing through our back bedroom window.

We enjoyed exploring homes that had been damaged by the bombs. They were uninhabitable and unsafe, but we were ignorant of the danger. Alfie Mack had a capful of small shrapnel bits.

'Wanna do a swap? I've some real shiny bits,' he said to Big Billy.

'Nah, my big shrapnel bits are much better than yours and worth more,' Big Billy replied.

I'd collect any wooden planks I could find in the debris. I'd chop them into little sticks which I'd place carefully in a small enamel bowl in a criss-cross pattern to make the bowl look full. Then I'd go from door to door to sell this as firewood. I became quite a sophisticated salesgirl, but my trick of making the bowl look full didn't always work: my customers would sometimes shake the bowl and tell me to come back when it was full.

'Come on luv, if you go away and fill it up, I'll buy two bowls. Go on, there's a good girl,' said Mrs Rumble. I was charging a penny a bowl and they wanted value for money! There were also many loose planks of wood from floorboards and rafters which I could chop up and sell. Collecting these also had its dangers, as they left great gaps in the floorboards below. At night, unbeknown to Mum, I would sit and take the splinters out of my hand with a sewing needle. There would always be another block of flats to try the next day, and people would always be interested in buying firewood as all the flats had fireplaces instead of central heating. Mum was always pleased with the money. 'That's wonderful – you are a good girl,' she'd say, which always gave me a glow as it made me feel important. Many Mondays, she went to the pawnshop with Dad's suit to raise money for the week. Somehow she always managed to get it back at the weekend if Dad came home on leave.

One weekend Dad came home unexpectedly. When he was able to get home, he liked to change out of his army uniform and into his only suit, but on this occasion, it was in the pawnshop. Mum told him she'd taken his suit to the cleaners.

'Kitty, come here quickly,' she whispered. 'Take this note up the road to number 20 and knock three times. Give her this note and wait for a little envelope.'

Mum was good at reading and writing. She told me to be polite to the woman, to smile when giving her the note and to ask her how her poor hands were. I found my way to number 20, a big house with high steps and a brass knocker that I could barely reach. After I'd waited a little while, a tiny grey-haired woman appeared. Her hands were wrinkled and bent over like claws, but she had rings on almost every finger. I handed over the note, keeping my distance, as she looked very strange. Undoing the crumpled note carefully, she read it and gave a big sigh.

'Wait here,' she said, and shut the door. After I'd waited for some time, she opened the door again and gave me a little envelope with money in it.

'Go straight home and give that to Mum,' she said. She was a moneylender and we often had to go to her, as well as the pawnshop, to borrow money. Out came Dad's suit from the pawnshop and thankfully he knew nothing about it. The next time, it was Mum's wedding ring that was pawned. When Dad noticed that Mum wasn't wearing it, she pretended she'd lost it down a drain while cleaning the porch. Mum sometimes owed the moneylender too much money, and had to wait for Dad's army pay before going back to her.

The bombing became even heavier. All schools were closed as it was too dangerous to travel there, and even when a school was opened, it was only for a few hours a week. As a result of this disruption, we had no formal education.

We listened to the wireless as often as we could, especially if our prime minister, Winston Churchill, was giving a speech. He gave us courage and hope.

A school in Canning Town where children were preparing to be re-evacuated took a direct hit during a day raid and over 400 children and teachers were killed. One night a bomb dropped down a ventilation shaft where many people were sheltering, and over 1,000 people were killed. Another tragedy happened in a Tube shelter in Bethnal Green. The shelter had a very narrow entrance. When the siren sounded, everyone rushed down the cramped staircase to get in. Someone tripped over at the bottom of the staircase and, as it was so dark, people fell on top of one another and were suffocated. Hundreds of people died. We later found out it wasn't even a real raid – the siren was just being tested.

Hetty and Mary had now left school and started work. On their first day, I painted their legs a tan colour with cold tea and drew a line up the back of each of their legs with a black pencil, to make it look like a stocking seam. They were going to look their best even though they didn't have real stockings. Now that they were working, they were able to help Mum with our finances. Once when a local shop had a supply of stockings, the queue was about two miles long – even longer than the queue for bananas, which another shop once managed to sell. I only saw bananas once during the war. Ships were needed to carry guns and tanks, not bananas. Rationing made life hard. So many food items were in short supply – butter, bacon, sugar, tea, meat and even sweets. Each person was issued with a ration book: beige for adults, blue for children and green for babies. Priority was given to babies for food such as oranges or bananas, although these were very rarely seen. Our family was registered for rations at the Sweet Shop.

Fruit was especially scarce.

'Mum, there's a queue at the shop – they might have some fruit. Give me Charlie's green ration book and I'll get in the queue for you,' I said to Mum one day. After waiting in the long queue for some time, I was allowed two large oranges and two bananas. That was all the fruit I'd seen throughout the war. It would be 1946 before I saw bananas again. Mum made the best of rationing and we never went hungry. There was lots of bread and Mum cooked potatoes and also dumplings.

Clothes were also rationed and we had special coupons to buy new items. This didn't worry us too much. In fact, it was a source of income for Mum, as she'd sell all our clothes coupons. Most people had to wear second-hand clothes. 'Make do and mend' became a wartime slogan. I no longer felt different wearing my sisters' overlarge clothes. Women did a good job at looking smart. Simple things like taking an old worn jumper, cutting off the sleeves and making winter mittens or woollen socks made the most of what we had. A smart sleeveless pullover could be made with the rest of the jumper. Nothing was wasted.

Chapter Ten

An adventure . . . and a tragedy

Mum was anxious about my wandering about all day, playing on the bomb sites with Billy. We were still in great danger from the falling debris and air raids. Sometimes we managed to get to school for the only hour it was open, but when the siren sounded, we had to run home to our shelters. Billy didn't always get back home in time before the 'all clear' had sounded. Poor Mum would be beside herself. The raids were now starting to happen more frequently during the day.

Climbing out of bed one morning, I noticed that Mum was looking worried.

'What's wrong, Mum?' I asked.

'I'm afraid you and Billy will have to be evacuated again,' she replied. She explained how concerned she was that Billy, now aged seven, was never around when the siren sounded. 'It won't be for long and I'll try to visit every weekend. It's just you and Billy this time. I know you'll look after him for me.'

'Oh no, I don't want to go and I certainly don't want to look after him,' I replied grudgingly. Grinning from ear to ear, Billy jumped out of bed, thrilled at the prospect of what he thought would be a wonderful adventure.

'Can I take my football?' he asked. His football took up all the space in his pillowcase.

'You can't take that – I'll buy you a new football when we get off the train,' I said.

'No, this is the only one that wins goals,' Billy insisted. I gave in and he went off with his football tucked under his arm, wiping his nose on the cuff of his sleeve.

'Don't do that – use your hanky and pull up your socks,' I commanded, taking charge already.

This time there seemed a lot less panic about being evacuated. As before, we all met up at the school. Now, knowing what to expect, I didn't mind being in charge of Billy, having been given permission to clip his ear if he misbehaved. But I knew that my responsibilities would deprive me of some of the freedom I'd previously enjoyed. For me, it wasn't going to be the adventure that Billy was looking forward to.

Alfie Mack and Big Billy were also being re-evacuated. 'Hi, boys!' said our Billy, as he swaggered up to them. Out came the football and everyone seemed happy.

Once again, the journey took some time but now everything seemed calmer. Billy was in awe of the train and the journey, and thankfully fell asleep after about half an hour. We'd had to get up so early that morning.

We finally arrived at our destination. As we stepped off the train, a fresh cool breeze brought the smell of the sea and we couldn't wait to dip our feet in the water. This was Hastings, a seaside resort on the south coast. We were excited, never having been to the seaside before.

There was no picking and choosing the children this time. We were met at the railway station by a woman with the now familiar WVS printed on her green hat.

'Hello dears,' she said, taking a look at our labels. 'Oh yes, come along with me. Here's a nice drink and some cake for you. Let's get in the car first.'

I grabbed hold of Billy and we happily followed the green hat. Alfie Mack and Big Billy had gone off together with a different WVS woman.

After a very short journey, we arrived at our new billet, which turned out to be a flat on the first floor of a small block, something I was used to. The woman who opened the green door immediately made us feel welcome. Mrs Kemp was large, with a smile that matched. We settled in quickly and were given our favourite meal of sausages and chips.

'Come on, let me show you to your room,' she said cheerfully.

Our new billet was clean, warm and comfortable. In our room there was a dressing table, a mirror and a small stool. The bed was so high that I had to lift Billy onto it.

It was early evening and still light outside, so we went to the seafront.

'Now make certain you come back soon,' said Mrs Kemp. She almost sounded like Mum, which was comforting.

At first, Billy was scared of the sea; as the tide came in, he ran away from it, wanting to know where the gates were to stop the water coming in any further. But after a few days, he couldn't keep away from the beach. He loved looking for shells, throwing stones into the sea and chasing the seagulls.

After a busy first day, we finally returned to our cosy room, fell into bed and slept soundly. Next morning, Mrs Kemp called out to Billy, asking him to come into her bedroom.

'Hello, Billy boy, just pop into my room for a moment,' she said. Excited, wondering what she had for him, he quickly put on his shoes, not bothering to tie his laces, and gently knocked on the door.

'Come on in,' she said. Walking in behind him, I heard her say, 'Pass me my leg.' Billy ran out of the room, screaming and shaking.

It turned out that she was disabled and had a wooden leg. After consoling Billy, I took her wooden leg from the corner of the room and placed it by her bedside, gently closing her door behind me as I left. It was her way of letting us know about her disability and why she wasn't able to do as much for us as she might have wanted. But we couldn't help wondering how she'd been able to put her leg in the corner of the room in the first place!

Since Billy was so afraid of Mrs Kemp, he clung to me constantly and wouldn't go near her. To make things easier for her, we were given a sandwich every day and told not to come back before six o'clock in the evening. When the weather was fine, we spent all day playing on the beach; when it rained, we sat in an ice cream parlour until we could return. School was never mentioned and naturally we never asked to go. We weren't unhappy; we loved the seaside and could always find something to do. There was also a small park nearby with swings and roundabouts, where we met up with other children.

Food and warmth were always there for us in the evening. But we missed our home and were constantly worried about the bombing in London. What would happen to us if our family were killed?

Early one morning a few months after our arrival, we were suddenly visited by a WVS woman who told us we were to be taken back to London.

'Is the war over?' I asked.

'No dear, but it won't be long and your mum wants you back right now.' No one would tell us why we had to go back home. As the WVS woman put us on a train, she instructed us, 'Now don't talk to anyone and don't get off until the end of the line in London. Someone will be there to meet you.' We tried to work out what we might have done wrong to upset Mrs Kemp.

We travelled alone with our labels tied onto our clothes. The journey back seemed much faster than the journey to Hastings. We were happy to be going home, but confused about the reason.

It was Hetty we saw first as the noisy train came to a halt at the station. It was wonderful to see my big sister. She gave me a big hug and a kiss. Billy didn't want to be kissed but was clearly happy to see Hetty. When we got home nothing much seemed to have changed, but Mum wasn't there.

'Where are Mum and little Charlie boy?' I asked.

Mary was sitting in the kitchen, looking worried. She didn't answer our questions and soon left the room.

'I've made you some salmon and shrimp paste sandwiches. Just eat them up. Mum won't be long,'

Hetty replied. Billy was starving and ate most of the sandwiches. I nibbled on one but couldn't understand why Mum was taking so long to get home.

'Charlie wasn't very well and Mum has taken him to hospital with a bad chest infection, which we think he caught from the damp of the shelter,' Hetty found the courage to tell me. 'The hospital told Mum he had whooping cough. He needed oxygen and has to stay in the hospital for a few nights.'

I missed Charlie almost as much as Mum and longed to see him. I wondered how much he'd grown and whether he'd still know me. He now had his own little cot with a beautiful knitted patchwork cover.

We'd arrived home at two in the afternoon, but it was now seven in the evening. What was taking Mum so long? At last, Mum arrived home, red-eyed and looking distraught.

'Where's Charlie?' I asked. With her face turned away, she struggled to tell me.

'Charlie had a coughing fit and couldn't breathe. Although he was given oxygen, he couldn't fight the infection and died in my arms,' Mum sobbed.

'No!' I screamed. Hetty and Mary hugged Mum and each other. The tears kept flowing. My beautiful baby. He was so very young. The thought of not holding him in my arms ever again was unbearable. We all sat in the kitchen, heads bowed, crying and holding onto one another – with Charlie's nappies hanging high, drying.

Dad, who was now abroad in the army, came home on compassionate leave for the funeral. Charlie was collected from the hospital and laid in a tiny white coffin which was kept in our front room on a table covered with a white sheet. He looked asleep. When I bent over to kiss him, he felt so cold that I fetched his pretty knitted cover and gently placed it over him.

A few days later, Dad carried Charlie's little coffin to the local church. As we walked out of our flat, all the neighbours came out on their balconies and stood by their doors to show their respect. It felt as if one big family was sharing our grief, despite their own personal problems and losses. Dressed in black clothes – some donated, some borrowed from our neighbours – we followed Dad. Mum had tried to dye some clothes black but it hadn't worked out, and the clothes came out green. After a short service, we walked to a waiting car and then on to the cemetery to say goodbye to our darling baby.

It was a deeply unhappy time for our family. Mum told me that Charlie was now a 'cherub' in heaven, looking after us, and I tried as best I could to believe her.

Chapter Eleven

Tables and chairs were suspended in mid-air

Bombs, including incendiary bombs, continued to fall on London as heavily as ever. The latter made the sky burn bright orange, with black clouds of smoke visible everywhere. The mournful wail of the siren continued night after night.

Billy, trembling and very afraid with his hands on his ears, would cry, 'Take it away, take it away!'

'Don't cry, we're all here and you're going to be fine,' Mum would try to console him, pulling him towards her and holding him tightly. He'd press his face into her apron, sobbing. Mum said he was so fearful because we'd lost Charlie.

'Come on, Billy. I've got some new comics for you

to look at,' I'd say, trying to prise him away from Mum as she was unable to move while he clung to her hips. We were still running down to our shelter every night and the noise was terrible.

Now there was a new fear of the pilotless V1 bombs, which fell night and day on London. They would swiftly scream across the sky before suddenly coming to a stop. Then they'd fall at an angle – so we knew that if one stopped directly above us, it wouldn't hit us and we'd probably be safe. If we heard one stop in the distance, we were terrified: there was every chance that the angle of its descent could bring it directly down onto us. Despite this, we tried to live life as normal. Most people had to walk to work because many of the roads were closed owing to unexploded bombs, called UXBs for short. Some days while out, I'd hear the sound of a rocket, but there was nothing I could do except put my hands over my ears and hope it would pass over somewhere else. It was dreadful to feel relieved that someone else was suffering and not you. When one of our family was out during a raid, we just prayed for their safe return.

The V1s were followed shortly after by an even deadlier bomb, the V2. These would arrive without the siren warning because the war cabinet didn't want Germany to know that they were reaching London, so we were left vulnerable to this terror. Many people died, both friends and neighbours. In just two weeks, 2,000 V1 bombs were launched, followed by the even deadlier V2s. We all lived in constant fear.

There were many direct hits on schools and homes. Nowhere was safe; even the shelters could get a direct hit and often did. One day Hetty came rushing home, her face white with fear: a V2 had just hit a Woolworths store in New Cross, killing over 100 people. As it was only a short distance from our home, we'd often go there.

'Stop shaking, you're safe now. Here, have a cup of tea,' Mum said to Hetty. Tea was Mum's cure for everything.

UXBs could explode hours or even days after dropping. One of these unexploded bombs landed on our block of flats. Coming up from our air raid shelter one morning after a heavy raid, we were told that we couldn't go back into our flats even to get fresh clothes. This really didn't bother us children, but it upset Mum. We spent the next few days in a rest centre – which was a school hall without beds, so we slept on the floor with nothing but blankets. We shared a cooker and a toilet with forty other families. Billy loved it as his friends were also in the hall. We were happy just to be alive. Some families had lost relatives and everything they owned.

Many people used underground stations for shelter after the trains had stopped running at night. One such shelter suffered a direct hit and many people were killed. Sometimes the casualties in one raid were so heavy that the area would simply be filled in as a communal grave, and a memorial plaque would be erected. This happened near us. A large shelter had been built in Kennington Park for families living in nearby flats. Billy and I used to enjoy playing in the park every day and when the shelter was hit, it was packed with over 200 people. It was just luck that Billy and I weren't playing in the park that day, as we most certainly would have used that shelter and been killed. The rescue work went on for days and the final death toll was 104, mainly women and children. Many of the bodies were unidentifiable.

The wailing of the siren and the constant bombing seemed to go on for ever. The smell of debris, dust and smoke filled the air. Many buildings that had been hit looked strangely distorted and eerie. Looking up at the houses, I sometimes saw half a room or the remains of someone's bedroom or front room. Tables and chairs were suspended in mid-air. Wallpaper hung down and flapped in the breeze. Many people were trapped in the debris of their own homes. I saw brave men and women digging to free them, not knowing if they would find corpses or people clinging to life. If people were trapped, doctors would do surgical operations there and then, and arms and legs were often amputated on the spot to save lives.

I played 'mums and dads' with my friends in these ruins, pretending that these half-rooms were our homes, oblivious of the danger we were putting ourselves in.

Chapter Twelve

Life in Blackpool was like a long holiday

Children who'd returned to London were left to find their own adventures, as schools were still closed. Some schools opened for an hour or so a day but if a siren was heard, the school would close at once. Mum wasn't happy for us to be out alone on our way to school, in case the siren started and we weren't able to get to a shelter before the bombs began to fall. For this reason, we didn't bother to go to school. None of us children were unhappy about this.

During the day, I often went to the local cinema, the Regal, with my friends. We always went in through the back door. This was more difficult for me as I always had to have Billy with me. As we didn't have any money, we'd gently force the door open and about five of us would creep in, bending down low. We'd quickly find vacant seats and keep our heads down so the usherette wouldn't see us. One or two of the boys were sometimes thrown out. Alfie was often dragged out by his collar, laughing because he knew he'd try to get in again almost immediately. The rest of us would sit and enjoy the film. I saw *Snow White and the Seven Dwarfs* many times, and also American child star Shirley Temple, singing 'On the Good Ship Lollipop'. Shirley had a head of blonde curls, and though I in contrast had a short black bob, this didn't stop me imitating her.

In the cinema, my special plan would be put into action when the usherette came along with her torch. I'd lean sideways towards the person sitting next to me and close my eyes, so the usherette would think that person was with me. This whole process of getting into the cinema and watching a film for free was known as 'bunking in'. But when a notice came up on the screen declaring, 'The siren has just sounded', we had to leave and run home as fast as we could. Many people would stay on, ignoring the siren, but I knew Mum would be worried if we didn't get to the shelter.

'Where have you been? I've been worried out of my life' was a regular phrase Mum used.

The bomb sites continued to be our playground. We knew no fear when playing hide and seek, despite the UXBs and the falling debris in the half-standing houses. 'Ready or not, here I come!' I'd call, clambering over bricks and rubble.

The raids continued. Mum was very worried about my roaming around the bomb sites with Billy and decided to send us away for the third time. She was particularly concerned about Billy, as when the siren sounded, he could seldom be found. He just didn't understand the danger, so she did what she thought was best for both of us. It was now 1943, and I was approaching thirteen and didn't want to go away again. Billy, now aged seven, was a real handful. Despite my objections, we were packed off. Even Billy wasn't so keen to be sent away again.

'None of my friends are going,' he complained. But in fact, his friends were at the school, ready to go when we arrived.

Once again, Billy and I joined a small group of children who were also being re-evacuated because of the V1 and V2 rockets. Although looking forward to the exciting train journey, I knew I was in for a busy time with Billy. The school organised the evacuation and we left prepared with our gas masks, pillowcases, and my new, and still unworn, pyjamas. I knew they might not fit me now, but I still treasured them. 'I could just lay them out on the bed for show,' I told Mum when she objected to my taking them away with me again.

The coach that took us to the mainline station was only half full this time, and on the train journey we fitted in like normal passengers. My only problem was that Billy was everywhere and it was so difficult to control him. We finally arrived at Blackpool, a busy seaside resort. There were numerous trains and so many people that it seemed almost as crowded as London. Within the crowds were many men in uniform, whom I later found out were Americans. Everyone was happy to see them, as we knew they were fighting on our side.

As we waited, we could already tell that Blackpool was full of fun. There were also miles and miles of beach. I held hands with Billy as we waited. 'Can we go to the beach now?' he asked, tugging at my skirt.

By this time, America had joined Britain in the war against Germany. In 1941, Japan had bombed an American base at Pearl Harbor, and as a result, America declared war on Japan. In response, Germany declared war on America. Americans were now fighting together with Britain. America was our friend and ally. They gave us a great deal of financial support, called Lend-Lease, which took Britain many years after the war to pay back.

We were soon met by a billeting officer, a jolly woman who seemed to be waiting just for us, which made us feel special. It was now about five o'clock. Again, there was no pointing and choosing this time. We were put straight into her car and taken to a house in a busy street. It was a big house with four floors. After a short wait, the door was opened by an attractive woman with a big smile. She had long black hair and was wearing a black dress with colourful flowers on it, long gold earrings and lots of shiny rings on every finger. She was very welcoming and we felt that everything was going to be fine for us this time around.

'Come on in, you poor little mites. My name's Nancy but you will call me Madam, just like all my friends do,' she said.

Billy was tugging on my arm. 'When can we go to the fair?' he asked. So much was going on in Blackpool and we could even hear the music from the doorstep we were standing on.

We were shown into a comfortable bedroom with a large double bed. It was warm and clean. There was a huge eiderdown on the bed and there were little lights above a dressing table. There was even a small bottle of perfume on it.

'I hope you'll find it comfortable and be happy with us,' Madam said warmly. What did she mean by *us*, I wondered, but I put this thought aside, as Billy couldn't wait to get out to the funfair. I was glad he wasn't missing home, but I knew I had a job on my hands keeping tabs on him. Mum had labelled all his clothes before we left, so every item had *Billy Baxter, London* on it. This gave me a little peace of mind.

'Come down when you're ready and I'll show you around,' Madam said. Dumping our pillowcases and gas masks, we went downstairs.

'Come on, Billy, let's try and get something to eat,' I suggested. Sitting on the stairs were two young women, beautifully dressed. One had long, wavy blonde hair, very red lips and a lovely smile.

'Hello, what's your name?' asked the girl with blonde hair.

'Hello, my name's Kitty and this is my brother, Billy,' I replied.

The other girl was busy painting her nails and just smiled. She had long curls and looked beautiful. We went into the kitchen and were told to help ourselves to anything we wanted. I made some jam sandwiches and tea.

Another young woman walked in. 'Oh, hi there, are you from London? I hope to go to London one day,' she said.

In the kitchen there was lots of food, including a huge piece of ham, masses of fruit and even sweets in little glass containers. I'd only seen ham like that hanging in shops, where if you were lucky, you might buy a slice. Where could it have come from with so much rationing?

'Can I have some of the sweets?' asked Billy, his eyes widening.

'You just go ahead and help yourself to anything you want,' said one of the girls. Billy grinned from ear to ear.

After eating our sandwiches, we were called into the sitting room, where there were three red-and-gold settees and matching curtains. The smell of perfume hung in the air. In this room were two more women talking to two American soldiers. I'd realised by now that five girls lived in the house and thought how nice it was to be in a big family like my own. The atmosphere was wonderful, as everyone was laughing and seemed so happy.

One of the soldiers looked at us and said, 'Well, gee, just look at that. So what's happening in London, guys?'

We just smiled. Would they ever believe us? As everyone seemed to be so happy, I decided not to spoil the moment by telling them about the bombs and people being killed every day.

Eventually Billy and I felt tired and went up to our room. We thought we were going to love staying in this house. We both fell asleep at once.

Next morning, we heard a gentle knocking on our door. Billy looked worried and clung tightly onto me.

'Who is it?' I asked. It was a jolly-looking woman who gently opened the door. She wore a gingham apron and said she was working in the kitchen.

'I'm sorry to wake you, but I'm so busy. Could you come down to help serve breakfast to our guests in the dining room?' she whispered. I dressed quickly and ran down to help, with Billy watching me. The guests were the American soldiers who'd been so kind to us the day before. They were pleased to see us and gave us chocolate and chewing gum. They even gave us some money.

'It's a tip,' they said, so we didn't complain. This was a real treat for us and we enjoyed helping the woman, who then cooked a great breakfast for us which we ate in the kitchen. This consisted of fried eggs, sausages and chips. We hadn't seen real eggs for months. Mum had only been able to give us the occasional dried powdered eggs from a tin. One egg each week per person was the ration in London, so we just accepted, speechless. After breakfast, we joined the girls and their American friends.

The Americans laughed at our cockney accents and wanted to know all about London. There were different Americans every morning, so we had plenty of talking to do. We loved chatting to the soldiers, as did the women who lived in the house, especially two called Francine and Paula. They looked like models, even first thing in the morning, when they came down to breakfast in their glamorous dressing gowns and joined the table. They were all very kind to us.

Billy and I went out to explore. Everything we could wish for was here – the beach, the Tower Ballroom and a wonderful funfair with the Big Dipper roller coaster on the seafront. There was also the Laughing Clown: you put a penny in the top of a statue of a clown who would then roll around, cackling with laughter, which made us laugh too. As we'd been given many pennies from the Americans back at the billet that morning, we had plenty of money to spend.

When we returned, the girls made a fuss of me, putting my hair in rollers and then into a fancy style. They even painted my nails bright red. I felt so special and grown-up. Paula told me that she really loved one of her American callers, named Hank, and that one day she hoped to marry him and go to live in America. Many girls wanted to do this and those who did were known as 'war brides'. Sadly, this wasn't always possible as many Americans had left wives and sweethearts behind.

The American visitors at the house were always happy and generous. They brought gifts of food or trinkets for the girls and would stay overnight. I loved dancing and they taught me to jive. 'OK, Kitty, let's have a twirl,' they'd say. In the afternoons, I'd sneak off to the Tower Ballroom, pretending to be older than my age. With my painted nails and the latest hairstyle that Paula had done so beautifully, it was easy for me to get in – no one ever asked my age. I was happy and wasn't worried about Billy, as I always knew where to find him. He was out most of the time, at the fairground in the Winter Gardens or playing on the fruit machines along the pier, and would always return when he ran out of money.

Life in Blackpool was like a long holiday that I could never have dreamt of back in London, with money, freedom, fun and dancing. I didn't realise that I might be in moral danger from the constant flow of American visitors at our billet. With my fancy hairstyle and painted nails, I looked very grown-up.

I knew I would soon have to get a job as fourteen was the legal age to work. Wondering why the young women didn't go out to work, I asked them if they had a job. They told me that they were paid to entertain the Americans and to make them feel happy and at home. This seemed to me a brilliant idea: with my lack of education, perhaps this would be a job I could do.

I wrote to Mum, explaining my idea about taking care of the American servicemen and telling her how much fun it was. I didn't understand why she arrived at the house in Blackpool to take us home so soon after receiving my letter, or why she was so angry with the billeting officer.

'Get your things at once. I'm taking you out of here!' she said. Both Billy and I protested that we wanted to stay, but Mum was furious. The girls hugged and kissed me when I left and I promised to go back and see them after the war. One day I did just that, but a block of flats stood in place of the house and there wasn't an American in sight. I was so sad to leave those kind girls who had been so good to Billy and me.

Chapter Thirteen

'Is that a letter from Dad?'

Although we'd enjoyed our Blackpool billet, it was good to be back home again, meeting up with my friend Joan, who was so grown-up and wearing red lipstick. 'I pinched it from my mum,' she explained.

Alfie Mack and Big Billy were banging on the door for our Billy, still wanting to play football. They didn't seem to have changed much; they'd just got taller.

The bombing continued and although it was less frequent, we still had to spend most nights in the shelter. It was a continuous nightmare. With so many people still being killed every night, the rescue team had a very hard job to do. Sometimes they'd have to collect the remnants of someone who'd been singing in a shelter only minutes before they were killed. The musty smell of debris hung around everywhere.

Alfie and Big Billy were getting little Billy into all sorts of trouble with their schemes to raise money, but Billy was happy being back home and out all day with his friends.

'Where have you been all day?' Mum would ask. With a shrug, he'd produce a handful of money from his pocket and count it out, telling her that he'd been doing odd jobs in the neighbourhood.

Billy and I now went to school for one or two hours a day, but we didn't learn much in that short time. Paper, pencil and books were still in short supply and we were quite happy about this. We were given homework but because we had to spend so much time in the shelter, it was impossible to do it. If we ever did manage to do it, it never got marked anyway so we ended up not even trying. Food and clothes and even furniture was still rationed. Furniture and clothes coupons interested us only because we could sell them.

Hetty had met a nice young man who was in the RAF and they planned to marry. She was given coupons to buy new so-called utility furniture, but this was very basic. In any case, she couldn't use these coupons. So many houses had been bombed that she couldn't find a home of her own, so she and her new husband would have to live in our flat. Our front room would become another bedroom. We hoped Hetty might find somewhere else to live before Dad returned from active service, as the front room was Dad's little haven where he would shut himself off to write or sleep after starting work so early.

Like all women aged eighteen years and over, Hetty and Mary were commissioned to do war work or join the forces. Mary joined the Women's Land Army and worked in agriculture, growing vegetables and taking care of animals, which meant she could go back to the countryside which she had enjoyed so much when evacuated. She would come home some weekends, looking smart in her uniform – a green jumper, fawn breeches and a dapper hat. Hetty went to work in a factory making shells for RAF planes. One weekend, Mary came home unexpectedly. I was wearing one of her dresses from our shared wardrobe. She was furious. 'Can't I have anything of my own in this house?' she shouted, as she threw all Hetty's and my clothes on the bed and locked the wardrobe door, taking the key away with her back to the country. That was the end of my dressing up for a while. Mum put our clothes into her big chest of drawers.

Dad was still fighting abroad. We didn't often hear from him and when we did, most of his letters were blocked out due to censorship. The army would go through all letters sent from war zones and black out any information that could be useful to the enemy. We weren't supposed to know where he was fighting. We only knew what the newspapers wanted to tell us. We missed him so much: his shiny shoes and only suit were always waiting for him to come home. We wrote to him every week, but it was difficult for him to write back because he was on a battlefield. It was such a lovely feeling when we did get a letter. How wonderful that he'd learnt to write. He'd tell us that it was snowing in Italy and to thank Mum for sending him the local paper, the *South London Press*. Despite the cost of postage, she did this every week. He told us how he shared it with his friends. He said he'd be home soon and signed his letters with rows of kisses for each of us. Mum's strength in all this continued to shine through. She was still working at her cleaning job, often having to walk there and back to save on tram fares.

The air raids were less frequent now and the news on the wireless was more positive. I understood that we were making rapid advances in Europe with the aid of the Russians and Americans moving in on two fronts in Germany. We were so looking forward to Dad coming home and all of us being together again, although poor Uncle Charlie was still fighting the Japanese in Burma.

One day in April, a few months after we'd returned from Blackpool, the postman dropped a letter through our front door.

'Is that a letter from Dad?' Mum enquired hopefully. I walked along the passage and picked it up.

'No, I don't think so, Mum. It's not from Dad.' It wasn't the familiar blue airmail letter, but a long brown envelope with the letters OHMS (On His Majesty's Service) printed on the outside. It looked very formal. I hoped Mum hadn't lost her cleaning job in the council office. Mum was busy getting the tea ready for Hetty and Mary. Mary had returned from the countryside on leave but they were both out shopping. Billy was playing outside so I was alone at home with Mum.

'Shall I open it for you?' I asked.

'Yes,' she answered, with her back to me. She was laying the table and, as always, making the meal look and taste interesting, despite the rationing. I opened the letter and read the awful words,

'It is with deep regret that I have to inform you of the death of your husband in the line of duty while on active service.'

I knew I had the dreadful job of reading that out to Mum. I was in shock and stood holding the letter, unable to say a word.

'Well, go on, read it – what's it about?' she asked.

'Oh, no, they've killed my dad,' I screamed and slowly read the letter out loud. Mum didn't turn round. I couldn't see her face, but knew she was crying. She smoothed the tablecloth.

'Let's have a cup of tea,' she said, still not turning round. On the second page of the letter there was a detailed account of how he'd died. He'd been badly wounded and had died the following day. *Was he conscious? Did he know what was happening?* These thoughts filled my head. Hetty and Mary returned home separately and Mum had to tell them individually about Dad. The sobbing went on all that day. When Billy was told, he couldn't really take in the fact that his father was gone for ever, Dad having been abroad for so long.

A few weeks later, the War Office sent us his army pay book and all the photos we'd sent him of us. The photos still showed the holes at the top where he'd pinned them up in his billet.

Another letter came for Mum a few days later, asking if she wanted to go to Italy to visit his grave. How stupid. She could hardly afford her fare to work. I was still in deep shock. Dad was buried in Italy. For us there were no goodbyes, no funeral, no closure.

Dad had been killed in the Battle of Monte Cassino. He was in a tank that went over a landmine, which blew up. This battle remains controversial. Did Dad and thousands of brave men die in vain? Could this battle have been avoided? Why did the army take that route? Was it simply to create a distraction? Did all these men go through that hell and die unnecessarily? So many questions still haunt me.

Only a few days earlier, we'd had such an uplifting letter from him, thanking us again for sending him the local paper and telling us to '*keep your chins up and I will see you soon*'. He never mentioned anything about the hell he was going through.

I stood outside the main gate of our flats. The woman in the corner shop saw me and called me inside. 'Here you are, dear, that's for you,' she said, handing me a bar of chocolate. The news must have already got to her. She meant well, but how could she think that this made up for the loss of my dad?

Just a few months later, I stood at our bedroom window, looking out onto a huge street party. All our friends and neighbours were enjoying cakes and sandwiches. Masses of food were piled high on long tables, food we hadn't seen for years. Everyone was singing and dancing and there were balloons everywhere. It was Victory in Europe, known as VE Day, the day on which people celebrated the end of the war in Europe. The whole country was celebrating. There were parties all over England.

'You're not going out there – we don't have anything to celebrate,' said Mum. My sisters agreed so we all stayed inside. There was to be no party for us. I looked up at Dad's suit hanging in the wardrobe, waiting for him to return. *What's to happen to that? What happens now?* At least I could console myself that I'd never have to be evacuated again. Three times had been enough. I could be with Mum and keep her company.

Meanwhile, we had letters from Uncle Charlie in Burma. Japan was finally forced to surrender when America dropped the atom bomb, first on Hiroshima and then on Nagasaki in 1945. Uncle Charlie came home safe and sound.

In September 1945 there was another, much happier, event in this memorable year – Hetty's colourful wedding with Mary and myself as bridesmaids. Everything we wore was borrowed, including Hetty's wedding dress. None of the bridesmaids wore matching dresses, so we called it a rainbow wedding.

The Sweet Shop helped out with cakes and gave us two bottles of wine, and all the neighbours made a food contribution. It was a great day.

This was also the month when, at the age of fourteen, I started work. Mum insisted I had to work in an office, so I found a job making tea at an advertising agency. I enjoyed working – I liked the company and the money. I'd walk all the way to Central London from home to save on tram fares, and happily gave Mum what I saved. It felt wonderful being a grown-up and a wage earner.

So a new life had begun for me. What did the future hold? Would I ever be able to put the war behind me, with the loss of my dear baby brother and loving father?

After a few months in my job, I was asked to work on the switchboard for an hour each day, to give me a break from my tea-making duties while the telephonist went to lunch. One day a handsome young man with blond hair, blue eyes and a most beautiful smile walked in to check on the switchboard. He was a telephone engineer, doing a regular check-up.

'Hello, has Irene gone to lunch? I'm just doing a routine check. What's your name?' he asked shyly.

He was so handsome and I felt my face burning so much that I knew I'd gone bright red.

'My name's Catherine, but everyone calls me Kitty,' I replied.

After checking the switchboard, he said, 'Well, Kitty, everything is in order here. Be back in a couple of months. By the way, I'm Leonard, but everyone calls me Len.' He smiled as he left. Only a week later he was back, when Irene was at lunch and I was again on the switchboard.

'Hello, Kitty, back again. Did I leave a screwdriver here last week?' he asked.

He searched around and as he leant across me to look for it, my heart seemed to miss a beat.

'Mmm, must have left it somewhere else. Sorry to have bothered you.'

Within a week, he was back again. 'Meant to ask you last week – would you like to come to the pictures with me? There's a great film on at the Odeon,' he said, while pretending to be looking for something in his bag. I was thrilled but tried not to show it. My first date.

We were married three years later when I was seventeen. A new chapter had begun.

Epilogue

After the war, my brother and sisters and I continued to live in our two-bedroom flat in Moffat House in Camberwell, but it quickly felt very crowded. Both my sisters got married and their husbands moved in with us too – accommodation was very hard to find at that time, because so much of London had been bombed and the city was rebuilding.

My eldest sister Hetty was always there for me, and I was devastated when she passed away in 2021.

My sister Mary and her family emigrated to Australia on the Ten Pound Pom scheme. We stayed in touch as much as possible, but over the years contact became less frequent.

My younger brother Billy went into the army for a while, just like our dad. He sadly died in his sixties, leaving behind a wife and daughters.

When I was seventeen, Len and I got married. We remained married for seven years – but having got together so young, we both felt the need to begin new lives alone, and went our separate ways.

I took a room in Brixton and a year after the separation, I met Remo. His family were in the catering business and he took a job in a café in Westminster, where I later joined him. Life was good. We had a flat above the café and raised our two daughters in the West End of London.

When Remo was diagnosed with Parkinson's disease and his condition began to deteriorate, he was forced to give up work. I encouraged him to return to Italy to the village he knew, where he could spend time with family and friends, and live an easier life. When his illness worsened further, he returned to London and he died surrounded by his family.

I continued to work in the café for many years before retiring at seventy-five, when I moved into a nearby flat.

I now keep myself busy writing, reading, sewing and knitting. For many years I have volunteered at the Imperial War Museum in Lambeth, where I give talks about my life as an evacuee to the public, and in particular to groups of schoolchildren. I also visit primary schools, where as part of their curriculum, I give talks to Year 6 students. I feel immensely humbled by the interest and genuine fascination that these children show in that period of my life.

A few years ago I visited my childhood home in Camberwell, and met the current residents. I don't imagine many people realise now that the railings, which have been replaced, were once used as makeshift stretchers; or that the mounds in the gardens hide the shelters where we used to take cover during air raids. I'd love for one of these shelters to be opened up as a memorial, as I feel it's vital that people know that they are not just part of the garden's landscape.

I hope my book goes some way in commemorating the life of a child during the Second World War, and will contribute to people's understanding of that time.

My heart goes out to anyone suffering in wars at the moment.

Acknowledgements

I would like to thank the following people who were instrumental in bringing *I'll Take That One* to publication:

Ngaire Bushell and the wonderful volunteers at the Imperial War Museum in Lambeth who encouraged me to write these memoirs.

My son-in-law, William Walton, who gave me his time and invaluable guidance.

Harry Andrews, who I met by chance in a London Square. We chatted about my memoirs which had started their journey as a record for friends and family. He immediately rang his friend, Susie Dunlop, the Publishing Director at Allison & Busby. My sincere thanks to you both, Harry and Susie.

Me talking to children at the Imperial War Museum, London, in 2022